The Complete Tefal Air Fryer Cookbook for Beginners 2024

Time-saving & Healthy Air Fryer Recipes for Enjoy Crispy Experience with Every Meal | UK Measurements & Ingredients

Reba B. Rivas

Copyright © 2024 Author Reba B. Rivas

Limitation of Liability/Disclaimer:

The publisher and author make no representations or warranties as to the accuracy or completeness of the contents of this work and expressly disclaim all warranties, including but not limited to warranties of fitness for a particular purpose. No warranty shall be made or enlarged in sales or promotional materials.

The advice and strategies contained herein may not be appropriate in every situation. In selling this work, the publisher may not offer medical, legal or other professional advice or services. If professional help is needed, the services of a competent professional should be sought. Neither the publisher nor the author shall be liable for damages resulting therefrom.

The mention of a person, organization or website in this work as a potential source of quotes and/or further information does not imply that the author or publisher endorses the information that may be provided by that person, organization or website or the advice they/it may give. suggestions they/it may have made. In addition, readers should be aware that the websites listed in this work may have changed or disappeared. In addition, readers should be aware that the websites listed in this work may have changed or disappeared between the time this work was written and the time it was read.

By using this recipe book, you agree to abide by the terms outlined in this copyright statement and disclaimer.

CONTENTS

INTRODUCTION 9
    Getting to know the Tefal Air Fryer 10
    Air Fryer vs Traditional Deep Frying 10
    Reasons to choose the Tefal Air Fryer Recipe Book 10
    Air Fryer Common Q&A 12

Bread And Breakfast Recipes 13
    Honey Oatmeal 13
    Light Frittata 13
    Farmers Market Quiche 13
    Holiday Breakfast Casserole 14
    Maple-peach And Apple Oatmeal 14
    English Scones 14
    Effortless Toffee Zucchini Bread 15
    Cajun Breakfast Potatoes 15
    Garlic Parmesan Bread Ring 15
    Breakfast Sausage Bites 16
    Breakfast Chimichangas 16
    Bagels With Avocado & Tomatoes 16
    Bacon & Egg Quesadillas 17
    Easy Vanilla Muffins 17
    Green Egg Quiche 17
    Mascarpone Iced Cinnamon Rolls 18
    Crunchy French Toast Sticks 18
    Broccoli Cornbread 19
    Apricot-cheese Mini Pies 19
    Green Onion Pancakes 19
    Goat Cheese, Beet, And Kale Frittata 20
    Ham And Cheddar Gritters 20
    Avocado Toasts With Poached Eggs 21
    Garlic Bread Knots 21
    Garlic-cheese Biscuits 21
    Egg & Bacon Pockets 21
    Breakfast Frittata 22
    Chocolate Almond Crescent Rolls 22
    Crunchy Granola Muffins 22
    Blueberry Pannenkoek (dutch Pancake) 23
    Apple French Toast Sandwich 23

Appetizers And Snacks Recipes 24
    Chili Pepper Popcorn 24
    Corn Dog Bites 24

Chicken Nachos	25
Bacon & Blue Cheese Tartlets	25
Cholula Avocado Fries	25
Homemade French Fries	25
Artichoke Samosas	26
Fried Pickles With Homemade Ranch	26
Chili Black Bean Empanadas	26
Antipasto-stuffed Cherry Tomatoes	27
Classic Chicken Wings	27
Cheese Arancini	27
Chili Corn On The Cob	28
Cauliflower "tater" Tots	28
Beef Steak Sliders	28
Avocado Toast With Lemony Shrimp	29
Asian Five-spice Wings	29
Charred Shishito Peppers	29
Hot Avocado Fries	30
Hot Shrimp	30
Breaded Mozzarella Sticks	30
Buffalo French Fries	31
Cheese Straws	31
Home-style Reuben Spread	31
Cinnamon Honeyed Pretzel Bites	31
Asian Rice Logs	32
Herby Breaded Artichoke Hearts	32
Hot Cheese Bites	32
Balsamic Grape Dip	33
Classic Potato Chips	33
Honey Tater Tots With Bacon	33

Vegetarian & Vegan Recipes 34

Ratatouille	34
Baked Aubergine Slices With Yogurt Dressing	34
Veggie Bakes	34
Aubergine Dip	34
Mushroom Pasta	35
Bagel Pizza	35
Lentil Balls With Zingy Rice	35
Air-fried Artichoke Hearts	35
Camembert & Soldiers	36
Sticky Tofu With Cauliflower Rice	36
Chickpea And Sweetcorn Falafel	36
Gnocchi Caprese	36
Broccoli Cheese	37
Mini Quiche	37
Rainbow Vegetables	37
Butternut Squash Falafel	37

Recipe	Page
Paneer Tikka	38
Sweet Potato Taquitos	38
Spring Ratatouille	38
Spinach And Egg Air Fryer Breakfast Muffins	38
Vegetarian "chicken" Tenders	39
Flat Mushroom Pizzas	39
Orange Zingy Cauliflower	39
Arancini	39
Spicy Spanish Potatoes	40
Courgette Burgers	40
Spinach And Feta Croissants	40
Roast Cauliflower & Broccoli	40
Lentil Burgers	40
Whole Wheat Pizza	41
Vegan Fried Ravioli	41

Beef, pork & Lamb Recipes 42

Recipe	Page
Crispy Pierogi With Kielbasa And Onions	42
Exotic Pork Skewers	42
Calzones South Of The Border	42
Baharat Lamb Kebab With Mint Sauce	43
Brie And Cranberry Burgers	43
Cheesy Mushroom-stuffed Pork Loins	44
Easy Carnitas	44
Carne Asada Recipes	44
Ground Beef Calzones	45
Better-than-chinese-take-out Sesame Beef	45
Authentic Sausage Kartoffel Salad	46
German-style Pork Patties	46
Crispy Pork Escalopes	46
Extra Crispy Country-style Pork Riblets	47
Greek Pita Pockets	47
Garlic-buttered Rib Eye Steak	47
Beef Al Carbon (street Taco Meat)	48
Chicken Fried Steak	48
Balsamic London Broil	48
Delicious Juicy Pork Meatballs	49
California Burritos	49
Glazed Meatloaf	49
Honey Mustard Pork Roast	50
Easy Tex-mex Chimichangas	50
Boneless Ribeye Steaks	51
Bacon-wrapped Filets Mignons	51
Aromatic Pork Tenderloin	51
Homemade Pork Gyoza	52
Barbecue Country-style Pork Ribs	52
Baby Back Ribs	52

Beef & Spinach Sauté 53

Fish And Seafood Recipes 53
　　Filled Mushrooms With Crab & Cheese 53
　　Dilly Red Snapper 53
　　Herb-rubbed Salmon With Avocado 54
　　Firecracker Popcorn Shrimp 54
　　Halibut With Coleslaw 54
　　Malaysian Shrimp With Sambal Mayo 55
　　Herby Prawn & Zucchini Bake 55
　　Horseradish Tuna Croquettes 55
　　Cheese & Crab Stuffed Mushrooms 56
　　Lime Bay Scallops 56
　　Almond Topped Trout 56
　　Flounder Fillets 56
　　Butternut Squash–wrapped Halibut Fillets 57
　　Easy-peasy Shrimp 57
　　Catalan-style Crab Samfaina 57
　　Horseradish Crusted Salmon 57
　　Herb-crusted Sole 58
　　King Prawns Al Ajillo 58
　　Garlic-lemon Steamer Clams 58
　　Coconut Shrimp Recipes 59
　　Crunchy Flounder Gratin 59
　　Chili Blackened Shrimp 59
　　Beer-breaded Halibut Fish Tacos 60
　　Classic Crab Cakes 60
　　Cilantro Sea Bass 60
　　Lobster Tails With Lemon Garlic Butter 61
　　Blackened Catfish 61
　　Halibut Quesadillas 61
　　Kid's Flounder Fingers 62
　　Home-style Fish Sticks 62
　　Hazelnut-crusted Fish 62

Poultry Recipes 63
　　Crunchy Chicken Tenders 63
　　Chicken Cordon Bleu 63
　　Christmas Chicken & Roasted Grape Salad 63
　　Herb-marinated Chicken 64
　　Chicken Adobo 64
　　Chilean-style Chicken Empanadas 64
　　Cajun Fried Chicken 64
　　Italian-inspired Chicken Pizzadillas 65
　　Cheesy Chicken Tenders 65
　　Chicken Souvlaki Gyros 65
　　Charred Chicken Breasts 66

Crispy Cornish Hen	66
Chicken And Cheese Chimichangas	66
Buffalo Chicken Wontons	66
Kale & Rice Chicken Rolls	67
Coconut Chicken With Apricot-ginger Sauce	67
Indian Chicken Tandoori	67
Italian Herb Stuffed Chicken	68
Chicken Flatbread Pizza With Spinach	68
Gruyère Asparagus & Chicken Quiche	68
Chicken Fried Rice	69
Honey Lemon Thyme Glazed Cornish Hen	69
Cajun Chicken Livers	69
Family Chicken Fingers	70
Asian-style Orange Chicken	70
Daadi Chicken Salad	70
Satay Chicken Skewers	71
Classic Chicken Cobb Salad	71
Chicken Tikka Masala	71
Fancy Chicken Piccata	72
Chicken Flautas	72

Vegetable Side Dishes Recipes 73

Roasted Brussels Sprouts With Bacon	73
Za'atar Bell Peppers	73
Cheese-rice Stuffed Bell Peppers	73
Green Dip With Pine Nuts	73
Truffle Vegetable Croquettes	74
Greek-inspired Ratatouille	74
Almond Green Beans	74
Veggie Fritters	75
Spiced Pumpkin Wedges	75
Goat Cheese Stuffed Portobellos	75
Glazed Carrots	76
Fried Corn On The Cob	76
Stuffed Avocados	76
Succulent Roasted Peppers	77
Yellow Squash	77
Buttery Radish Wedges	77
Toasted Choco-nuts	77
Fried Green Tomatoes With Sriracha Mayo	78
Stunning Apples & Onions	78
Mexican-style Roasted Corn	78
Mashed Potato Tots	79
Fried Pearl Onions With Balsamic Vinegar And Basil	79
Bacon-wrapped Asparagus	80
Fried Cauliflower With Parmesan Lemon Dressing	80
Fried Eggplant Balls	80

Baked Shishito Peppers 81
Spiced Roasted Acorn Squash 81
Tofu & Broccoli Salad 81
Hot Okra Wedges 81
Italian Breaded Eggplant Rounds 82
Charred Radicchio Salad 82

Desserts Recipes 83

Lemon Buns 83
Apple And Cinnamon Puff Pastry Pies 83
New York Cheesecake 83
Cherry Pies 84
Grain-free Millionaire's Shortbread 84
Chocolate And Berry Pop Tarts 84
Mini Egg Buns 85
Banana Maple Flapjack 85
Sweet Potato Dessert Fries 85
Thai Fried Bananas 85
Pop Tarts 86
Chocolate Soufflé 86
Coffee, Chocolate Chip, And Banana Bread 86
Peanut Butter & Chocolate Baked Oats 87
Apple And Cinnamon Empanadas 87
Shortbread Cookies 87
Pecan & Molasses Flapjack 87
Sugar Dough Dippers 87
Oat-covered Banana Fritters 88
Chocolate Orange Fondant 88
Apple Crumble 88
Lemon Pies 88
Lemon Tarts 89
Brazilian Pineapple 89
Apple Chips With Yogurt Dip 89
Banana And Nutella Sandwich 89
Crispy Snack Apples 89
Strawberry Danish 90
Birthday Cheesecake 90
Grilled Ginger & Coconut Pineapple Rings 90
Lava Cakes 90

APPENDIX A: Measurement 91

APPENDIX B: Recipes Index 93

INTRODUCTION

Reba B. Rivas is a seasoned culinary professional with a rich background in the culinary arts. With over twenty years of experience in the food industry, Reba has mastered the art of cooking and developed a profound passion for creating delectable dishes.

Her journey as the author of the Tefal Air Fryer Cookbook was a labor of love. She dedicated countless hours to perfecting each recipe, drawing from her extensive culinary knowledge to ensure that every dish not only tasted exceptional but was also approachable for home cooks of all levels.

Reba's career began in the bustling kitchens of renowned restaurants, where she worked alongside top chefs, mastering the intricacies of culinary techniques and flavor profiles. This invaluable experience laid the foundation for her to become a culinary expert in her own right.

Throughout her career, Reba recognized the growing need for practical yet delicious recipes that fit into the busy lives of everyday home cooks. Her background as a professional chef uniquely positioned her to bridge the gap between restaurant-quality cuisine and home cooking, and this cookbook is a testament to her commitment to making gourmet meals accessible to all.

Beyond her culinary skills, Reba is a health-conscious chef who understands the importance of balanced and nutritious meals. Her Tefal Air Fryer Cookbook not only delivers on flavor but also emphasizes healthier cooking methods, making it a valuable resource for individuals seeking both taste and well-being in their meals.

In summary, Reba B. Rivas's Tefal Air Fryer Cookbook is a culmination of her extensive culinary expertise, dedication to simplifying gourmet cooking, and commitment to promoting healthier eating. Her passion for the culinary arts shines through in every recipe, making this cookbook a must-have for anyone looking to elevate their cooking skills with the Tefal Air Fryer.

Getting to know the Tefal Air Fryer

The Tefal Air Fryer is a cutting-edge kitchen appliance that revolutionizes cooking by utilizing advanced hot air circulation technology to provide a healthier and more efficient alternative to traditional frying methods. This innovative device allows users to prepare a wide range of dishes, from crispy snacks to succulent mains and even delectable desserts, using significantly less oil than deep frying. It ensures that food is evenly cooked and achieves a crispy texture, all while reducing calorie and fat content, making it an excellent choice for health-conscious individuals. The Tefal Air Fryer also boasts user-friendly controls and versatility, making it a valuable addition to any kitchen, simplifying meal preparation, and promoting a more wholesome approach to cooking.

Air Fryer vs Traditional Deep Frying

Aspect	Air Frying	Traditional Deep Frying
Cooking Method	Uses hot air circulation to cook food evenly.	Immerses food in hot oil for frying.
Oil Usage	Requires significantly less oil, typically 70-80% less than deep frying.	Uses a substantial amount of oil for frying.
Health Benefits	Results in lower fat and calorie content in dishes.	Dishes tend to be higher in fat and calories due to oil absorption.
Texture	Achieves a crispy texture similar to deep frying without excessive oil.	Creates a crispy texture due to oil absorption.
Cooking Time	Cooks food relatively quickly due to high heat circulation.	Cooking times can be longer due to oil heat transfer.
Cleanup	Easier cleanup as there is no large amount of hot oil to dispose of.	Cleanup can be more involved due to oil disposal and potential splatter.
Versatility	Can cook a variety of foods, from snacks to main courses and desserts.	Mainly used for frying foods, limiting versatility.

Reasons to choose the Tefal Air Fryer Recipe Book

Tailored for Tefal Air Fryers

This recipe book is specifically designed for Tefal Air Fryers, ensuring that the recipes are optimized for these appliances, resulting in perfect cooking results every time.

Expertly Crafted Recipes

The cookbook features a curated selection of expertly crafted recipes that cater to a wide range of tastes and preferences, from savory dishes to sweet treats.

Healthy Cooking

Tefal is known for promoting healthier cooking methods, and this cookbook aligns with that ethos by offering recipes that require less oil, making it an excellent choice for those looking to reduce their fat intake.

Easy-to-Follow Instructions

The recipes are accompanied by clear and concise instructions, making them accessible to both experienced cooks and beginners. You can confidently create restaurant-quality dishes in your own kitchen.

Varied Selection

The cookbook includes a diverse range of recipes, ensuring that you have plenty of options to choose from for everyday meals, special occasions, or culinary adventures.

Time Efficiency

Many recipes in the cookbook are designed to save you time without compromising on flavor, making it ideal for busy individuals and families.

Nutritional Information

The cookbook often provides nutritional information for each recipe, allowing you to make informed dietary choices.

Inspiration

Whether you're seeking inspiration for quick weekday meals or planning a special dinner, this cookbook provides a wealth of ideas and possibilities.

Tefal Quality Assurance

As an official Tefal cookbook, it carries the assurance of a reputable brand known for its quality kitchen appliances and culinary expertise.

Versatile Cooking

Tefal Air Fryers are versatile appliances, and this cookbook maximizes their potential by offering a wide array of recipes, from appetizers to main courses and desserts.

Air Fryer Common Q&A

1. What types of food can I cook in an air fryer?

Air fryers are versatile and can cook a wide range of foods, including but not limited to french fries, chicken wings, vegetables, seafood, frozen foods, and even desserts like pastries and cookies.

2. Can I use my regular recipes in an air fryer?

You can adapt many regular recipes for the air fryer, but you may need to make adjustments to cooking times and temperatures. Recipes specifically designed for air frying often yield the best results.

3. Are air fryers easy to clean?

Many air fryer baskets and trays have non-stick coatings and are dishwasher-safe, making cleanup relatively easy. However, it's essential to clean the components thoroughly after each use to maintain performance.

4. Can I use aluminum foil or parchment paper in the air fryer?

Yes, you can use aluminum foil or parchment paper in the air fryer, but be cautious not to cover the entire basket or block the air circulation. These materials can help prevent food from sticking to the basket.

5. Do air fryers produce any smoke or odors?

Air fryers generally produce minimal smoke and odors compared to traditional deep frying. However, some cooking odors may be noticeable, especially when preparing strongly aromatic foods.

6. Can I preheat an air fryer?

Yes, preheating the air fryer for a few minutes before adding food can help achieve more consistent cooking results, especially for certain recipes.

7. Are there any safety precautions when using an air fryer?

Yes, it's essential to follow safety guidelines, such as avoiding overcrowding the basket, using oven mitts when handling hot components, and ensuring the appliance is placed on a stable, heat-resistant surface.

Bread And Breakfast Recipes

Honey Oatmeal

Servings: 6
Cooking Time: 35 Minutes
Ingredients:
- 2 cups rolled oats
- 2 cups oat milk
- ¼ cup honey
- ½ cup Greek yogurt
- 1 tsp vanilla extract
- ½ tsp ground cinnamon
- ¼ tsp salt
- 1 ½ cups diced mango

Directions:
1. Preheat your air fryer to 380°F (193°C).
2. In a large bowl, combine the rolled oats, oat milk, honey, Greek yogurt, vanilla extract, ground cinnamon, and salt. Stir these ingredients together until they are well combined.
3. Gently fold in ¾ cup of the diced mango into the oatmeal mixture.
4. Grease a cake pan or suitable oven-safe dish and pour the oatmeal mixture into it. Make sure it's spread evenly.
5. Sprinkle the remaining ¾ cup of diced mango on top of the oatmeal mixture.
6. Place the cake pan with the oatmeal mixture into the preheated air fryer.
7. Air fry the oatmeal for 30 minutes or until it's set and the top has a nice golden color.
8. Once done, let it cool for about 5 minutes before serving.
9. Serve your Honey Oatmeal and enjoy a delicious and healthy breakfast!

Light Frittata

Servings: 4
Cooking Time: 25 Minutes
Ingredients:
- ½ red bell pepper, chopped
- 1 shallot, chopped
- 1 baby carrot, chopped
- 1 tbsp olive oil
- 8 egg whites
- 1/3 cup milk
- 2 tsp grated Parmesan cheese

Directions:
1. Preheat your air fryer to 350°F (175°C).
2. In a baking pan, combine the chopped red bell pepper, shallot, baby carrot, and olive oil. Toss them together to coat the vegetables evenly.
3. Place the baking pan with the vegetables into the preheated air fryer.
4. Bake the vegetables for about 4-6 minutes, or until they become soft. You can shake the basket once during cooking to ensure even cooking.
5. While the vegetables are cooking, whisk the egg whites in a separate bowl until they become fluffy. Then, stir in the milk.
6. Once the vegetables are soft, pour the egg white and milk mixture over the cooked vegetables in the baking pan.
7. Sprinkle the grated Parmesan cheese on top of the mixture.
8. Return the pan to the air fryer and bake for an additional 4-6 minutes, or until the frittata has puffed up and is cooked through.
9. Carefully remove the pan from the air fryer (it will be hot), and let the frittata cool for a minute or two.
10. Slice the Light Frittata into portions and serve. Enjoy your healthy and delicious frittata!

Farmers Market Quiche

Servings: 4
Cooking Time: 35 Minutes
Ingredients:
- 4 button mushrooms
- 1/4 medium red bell pepper
- 5 ml extra-virgin olive oil
- One 9-inch pie crust, at room temperature
- 60 ml grated carrot
- 60 ml chopped fresh baby spinach leaves
- 3 eggs, whisked
- 60 ml half-and-half
- 1/2 teaspoon thyme
- 1/2 teaspoon sea salt
- 57 grams crumbled goat cheese or feta

Directions:
1. In a medium bowl, toss the mushrooms and red bell pepper with extra-virgin olive oil. Place them into the air fryer basket.
2. Set the temperature to 200°C (400°F) for 8 minutes, stirring after 4 minutes. Remove the mushrooms and bell peppers from the air fryer and roughly chop them. Wipe the air fryer clean.

3. Prepare a 7-inch oven-safe baking dish by spraying the bottom with cooking spray.
4. Place the pie crust into the baking dish and fold over the edges, crimping them or using a fork to give them some shape.
5. In a medium bowl, mix together the chopped mushrooms, bell peppers, grated carrot, chopped spinach, and eggs.
6. Stir in the half-and-half, thyme, and sea salt.
7. Pour the quiche mixture into the prepared pie crust.
8. Top the quiche with crumbled goat cheese or feta.
9. Place the quiche into the air fryer basket.
10. Set the temperature to 165°C (325°F) for 30 minutes.
11. When the cooking is complete, turn the quiche halfway and cook for an additional 5 minutes.
12. Allow the quiche to rest for 20 minutes before slicing and serving.

Holiday Breakfast Casserole

Servings: 2
Cooking Time: 25 Minutes
Ingredients:
- 60g cooked spicy breakfast sausage
- 5 eggs
- 30ml (2 tbsp) heavy cream
- 1.25ml (1/2 tsp) ground cumin
- Salt and pepper, to taste
- 60g feta cheese crumbles
- 1 tomato, diced
- 1 can green chiles, including juice
- 1 zucchini, diced

Directions:
1. Preheat your air fryer to 163°C (325ºF).
2. In a mixing bowl, combine all the ingredients - cooked spicy breakfast sausage, eggs, heavy cream, ground cumin, salt, pepper, feta cheese crumbles, diced tomato, green chiles (including juice), and diced zucchini.
3. Pour the mixture into a greased baking pan.
4. Place the baking pan in the frying basket of your air fryer.
5. Bake for 14 minutes in the preheated air fryer.
6. Let it cool for 5 minutes before slicing.
7. Serve your Holiday Breakfast Casserole right away. Enjoy!

Maple-peach And Apple Oatmeal

Servings: 4
Cooking Time: 15 Minutes
Ingredients:
- 2 cups old-fashioned rolled oats
- ½ tsp baking powder
- 1 ½ tsp ground cinnamon
- ¼ tsp ground flaxseeds
- ⅛ tsp salt
- 1 ¼ cups vanilla almond milk
- ¼ cup maple syrup
- 1 tsp vanilla extract
- 1 peeled peach, diced
- 1 peeled apple, diced

Directions:
1. Preheat your air fryer to 350°F (175°C).
2. In a large bowl, combine the rolled oats, baking powder, ground cinnamon, ground flaxseeds, and salt.
3. Stir in the vanilla almond milk, maple syrup, and vanilla extract until all the ingredients are well combined.
4. Add ¾ of the diced peaches and ¾ of the diced apples to the oatmeal mixture. Stir to distribute the fruit evenly.
5. Grease 6 ramekins or small oven-safe dishes to prevent sticking.
6. Divide the oatmeal mixture evenly between the greased ramekins.
7. Place the filled ramekins in the air fryer basket, ensuring there is some space between them.
8. Air-fry the oatmeal at 350°F for 8-10 minutes, or until the top is golden and the oatmeal is set.
9. Carefully remove the ramekins from the air fryer and let them cool for a minute or two.
10. Garnish each serving with the remaining diced peaches and apples.
11. Serve the Maple-Peach and Apple Oatmeal warm, right from the air fryer.

English Scones

Servings: 8
Cooking Time: 8 Minutes
Ingredients:
- 250 grams all-purpose flour
- 15 ml baking powder
- 2.5 ml salt
- 30 grams sugar
- 60 grams unsalted butter
- 160 ml plus 15 ml whole milk, divided

Directions:
1. Preheat the air fryer to 190°C (380°F).
2. In a large bowl, whisk together the all-purpose flour, baking powder, salt, and sugar.
3. Using a pastry blender or your fingers, cut in the unsalted butter until you have pea-sized crumbles.

4. Create a well in the center of the mixture and pour in 160 ml of the whole milk.
5. Quickly mix the batter until a ball of dough forms. Knead the dough three times.
6. Place the dough onto a floured surface and use your hands or a rolling pin to flatten it until it's about 2 cm (3/4 inch) thick.
7. Use a biscuit cutter or drinking glass to cut out 10 circles from the dough, reusing and flattening the dough as needed to use up all the batter.
8. Lightly brush the tops of the scones with the remaining 15 ml of whole milk.
9. Place the scones into the air fryer basket.
10. Cook for 8 minutes or until the scones are golden brown and cooked in the center.

Effortless Toffee Zucchini Bread

Servings: 6
Cooking Time: 30 Minutes
Ingredients:
- 120 grams flour
- 1/2 tsp baking soda
- 100 grams granulated sugar
- 1/4 tsp ground cinnamon
- 1/4 tsp nutmeg
- 1/4 tsp salt
- 85 grams grated zucchini
- 1 large egg
- 15 ml olive oil
- 5 ml vanilla extract
- 30 grams English toffee bits
- 30 grams mini chocolate chips
- 60 grams chopped walnuts

Directions:
1. Preheat the air fryer to 190°C (375°F).
2. In a bowl, combine the flour, baking soda, toffee bits, granulated sugar, ground cinnamon, nutmeg, salt, grated zucchini, egg, olive oil, vanilla extract, and chocolate chips.
3. Add the chopped walnuts to the batter and mix until they are evenly distributed.
4. Grease a cake pan.
5. Pour the batter into the greased cake pan.
6. Place the cake pan in the air fryer.
7. Bake for 20 minutes or until a toothpick inserted into the center comes out clean.
8. Allow the bread to sit for 10 minutes until it has slightly cooled.
9. Slice and serve immediately.

Cajun Breakfast Potatoes

Servings: 4
Cooking Time: 20 Minutes
Ingredients:
- 450g roasting potatoes (like russet), scrubbed clean
- 15ml vegetable oil
- 2g paprika
- 0.5g garlic powder
- 0.25g onion powder
- 0.25g ground cumin
- 5g thyme
- 5g sea salt
- 2.5g black pepper

Directions:
1. Cut the potatoes into 2.5cm cubes.
2. In a large bowl, toss the cut potatoes with vegetable oil.
3. Sprinkle paprika, garlic powder, onion powder, cumin, thyme, salt, and pepper onto the potatoes, and toss to coat them evenly.
4. Preheat the air fryer to 200°C (400°F) for 4 minutes.
5. Add the seasoned potatoes to the air fryer basket and air fry for 10 minutes. Stir or toss the potatoes to ensure even cooking and continue air frying for an additional 5 minutes. Stir or toss again and continue air frying for another 5 minutes or until the desired crispness is achieved.

Garlic Parmesan Bread Ring

Servings: 6
Cooking Time: 30 Minutes
Ingredients:
- 115 grams unsalted butter, melted
- A pinch of salt (omit if using salted butter)
- 85 grams grated Parmesan cheese
- 3 to 4 cloves garlic, minced
- 15 ml chopped fresh parsley
- 454 grams frozen bread dough, defrosted
- Olive oil
- 1 egg, beaten

Directions:
1. Combine the melted butter, a pinch of salt (if using unsalted butter), Parmesan cheese, minced garlic, and chopped parsley in a small bowl.
2. Roll the dough out into a rectangle that measures approximately 20 cm by 43 cm (8 inches by 17 inches).
3. Spread the butter mixture over the dough, leaving a half-inch border un-buttered along one of the long edges.
4. Roll the dough from one long edge to the other, ending with the un-buttered border. Pinch the seam shut tightly.

5. Shape the log into a circle, sealing the ends together by pushing one end into the other and stretching the dough around it.

6. Cut out a circle of aluminum foil that is the same size as the air fryer basket. Brush the foil circle with oil and place an oven-safe ramekin or glass in the center.

7. Transfer the dough ring to the aluminum foil circle, around the ramekin. This will help you make sure the dough will fit in the basket and maintain its ring shape.

8. Use kitchen shears to cut 8 slits around the outer edge of the dough ring halfway to the center. Brush the dough ring with egg wash.

9. Preheat the air fryer to 200°C (400°F) for 4 minutes. When it has preheated, brush the sides of the basket with oil and transfer the dough ring, foil circle, and ramekin into the basket.

10. Slide the drawer back into the air fryer, but do not turn the air fryer on. Let the dough rise inside the warm air fryer for 30 minutes.

11. After the bread has proofed in the air fryer for 30 minutes, set the temperature to 170°C (340°F) and air-fry the bread ring for 15 minutes.

12. Flip the bread over by inverting it onto a plate or cutting board and sliding it back into the air fryer basket.

13. Air-fry for another 15 minutes.

14. Let the bread cool for a few minutes before slicing the bread ring in between the slits and serving it warm.

Breakfast Sausage Bites

Servings: 4
Cooking Time: 30 Minutes
Ingredients:
- 450g ground pork sausages
- 60ml diced onions
- 5ml rubbed sage
- 1.25ml ground nutmeg
- 2.5ml fennel
- 1.25ml garlic powder
- 30ml parsley, chopped
- Salt and pepper to taste

Directions:
1. Preheat your air fryer to 175°C (350°F).
2. In a bowl, combine all ingredients except the parsley.
3. Form the mixture into balls.
4. Place the sausage balls in the greased air fryer basket.
5. Air Fry for 10 minutes, flipping them once during cooking.
6. Sprinkle with chopped parsley and serve immediately.
7. Enjoy your Breakfast Sausage Bites!

Breakfast Chimichangas

Servings: 4
Cooking Time: 8 Minutes
Ingredients:
- Four 8-inch flour tortillas
- 120ml canned refried beans
- 240ml scrambled eggs
- 120ml grated cheddar or Monterey jack cheese
- 15ml vegetable oil
- 240ml salsa

Directions:
1. Lay the flour tortillas out flat on a cutting board.
2. In the center of each tortilla, spread 30ml (2 tablespoons) of refried beans.
3. Next, add 60ml (1/4 cup) of scrambled eggs and 30ml (2 tablespoons) of cheese to each tortilla.
4. To fold the tortillas, begin on the left side and fold to the center. Then, fold the right side into the center. Next, fold the bottom and top down and roll over to completely seal the chimichanga.
5. Using a pastry brush or oil mister, brush the tops of the tortilla packages with oil.
6. Preheat your air fryer to 200°C (400°F) for 4 minutes.
7. Place the chimichangas into the air fryer basket, seam side down, and air fry for 4 minutes.
8. Using tongs, turn over the chimichangas and cook for an additional 2 to 3 minutes or until they are light golden brown.
9. Serve your delicious Breakfast Chimichangas with salsa.
10. Enjoy your meal!

Bagels With Avocado & Tomatoes

Servings: 2
Cooking Time: 35 Minutes
Ingredients:
- 80g all-purpose flour
- 1/2 tsp active dry yeast
- 80g Greek yogurt
- 8 cherry tomatoes
- 1 ripe avocado
- 1 tbsp lemon juice
- 2 tbsp chopped red onions
- Black pepper to taste

Directions:
1. Preheat your air fryer to 200°C (400°F).
2. In a mixing bowl, combine the all-purpose flour, active dry yeast, and Greek yogurt. Mix until you have a smooth dough, adding more flour if needed. Divide the dough into 2 equal portions.

3. Using a rolling pin, roll each portion into a 23cm (9-inch) long strip. Form a ring with each strip and press the ends together to create 2 bagels.
4. In a bowl of hot water, soak the bagels for 1 minute. Then, shake off the excess water and let them rise for 15 minutes in the air fryer.
5. After the rising time, bake the bagels for 5 minutes, then turn them over, top with cherry tomatoes, and bake for another 5 minutes.
6. While the bagels are baking, prepare the avocado spread. Cut the avocado in half, discard the pit, and scoop the flesh into a bowl. Mash it with a fork and stir in the lemon juice and chopped red onions.
7. Once the bagels are done, allow them to cool slightly and then cut them in half. Spread each half with the avocado mixture, top with 2 slices of baked tomatoes, and sprinkle with black pepper.
8. Serve your delicious Bagels with Avocado & Tomatoes immediately. Enjoy!

Bacon & Egg Quesadillas

Servings: 4
Cooking Time: 30 Minutes
Ingredients:
- 8 flour tortillas
- 225g cooked bacon, crumbled
- 6 eggs, scrambled
- 1 1/2 cups grated cheddar cheese
- 1 tsp chopped chives
- 1 tsp parsley
- Black pepper to taste

Directions:
1. Preheat your air fryer to 180°C (350°F).
2. Place one tortilla in the bottom of a cake pan.
3. Spread 1/4 portion of the crumbled bacon, scrambled eggs, chopped chives, parsley, black pepper, and grated cheddar cheese evenly over the tortilla.
4. Top with a second tortilla to create a quesadilla sandwich.
5. Place the cake pan in the air fryer basket and bake for 4 minutes until the quesadilla is golden and the cheese is melted.
6. Carefully remove the quesadilla from the air fryer and set it aside on a large plate.
7. Repeat the process with the remaining ingredients to make additional quesadillas.
8. Allow the quesadillas to cool for 3 minutes before slicing them.
9. Serve your delicious bacon and egg quesadillas right away. Enjoy!

Easy Vanilla Muffins

Servings: 6
Cooking Time: 35 Minutes + Cooling Time
Ingredients:
- 160 grams flour
- 70 grams butter, melted
- 55 grams brown sugar
- 30 grams raisins
- 1/2 teaspoon ground cinnamon
- 70 grams granulated sugar
- 60 ml milk
- 1 large egg
- 5 ml vanilla extract
- 5 grams baking powder
- Pinch of salt

Directions:
1. Preheat the air fryer to 165°C (330°F).
2. In a bowl, combine 80 grams of flour, 35 grams of melted butter, brown sugar, and ground cinnamon. Mix until the mixture becomes crumbly. Set this mixture aside.
3. In another bowl, combine the remaining melted butter, granulated sugar, milk, egg, and vanilla extract. Stir until well combined.
4. Add the remaining flour (80 grams), baking powder, raisins, and a pinch of salt to the wet ingredients. Stir until the batter is well combined.
5. Spray 6 silicone muffin cups with baking spray.
6. Spoon half of the muffin batter into the muffin cups.
7. Sprinkle a teaspoon of the cinnamon mixture over the batter in each cup.
8. Add the remaining muffin batter on top of the cinnamon mixture.
9. Sprinkle the remaining cinnamon mixture on top of the muffins, gently pressing it into the batter.
10. Place the muffin cups in the air fryer basket.
11. Bake for 14-18 minutes or until a toothpick inserted into the center of a muffin comes out clean.
12. Allow the muffins to cool for 10 minutes, then remove them from the cups.
13. Serve and enjoy your Easy Vanilla Muffins!

Green Egg Quiche

Servings: 4
Cooking Time: 30 Minutes
Ingredients:
- 240 grams broccoli florets

- 160 grams baby spinach
- 2 garlic cloves, minced
- 1.25 ml ground nutmeg
- 15 ml olive oil
- Salt and pepper to taste
- 4 eggs
- 2 scallions, chopped
- 1 red onion, chopped
- 15 ml sour cream
- 120 grams grated fontina cheese

Directions:
1. Preheat the air fryer to 190°C (375°F).
2. Combine broccoli, baby spinach, red onion, minced garlic, ground nutmeg, olive oil, and salt in a medium bowl, tossing to coat. Arrange the broccoli in a single layer in a parchment-lined frying basket and cook for 5 minutes. Remove and set aside.
3. Use the same medium bowl to whisk eggs, salt, pepper, chopped scallions, and sour cream. Add the roasted broccoli and 60 grams of fontina cheese, then mix until all ingredients are well combined.
4. Pour the mixture into a greased baking dish and top with the remaining 60 grams of fontina cheese.
5. Bake in the air fryer for 15-18 minutes until the center is set.
6. Serve and enjoy your Green Egg Quiche with the UK units provided in the recipe!

Mascarpone Iced Cinnamon Rolls

Servings: 6
Cooking Time: 40 Minutes
Ingredients:
- For the Cinnamon Rolls:
- ¼ cup mascarpone cheese, softened
- 9 oz puff pastry sheet
- 3 tbsp light brown sugar
- 2 tsp ground cinnamon
- 2 tsp butter, melted
- For the Icing:
- ¼ tsp vanilla extract
- ¼ tsp salt
- 2 tbsp milk
- 1 tbsp lemon zest
- ¼ cup confectioners' sugar

Directions:
1. Preheat your air fryer to 320°F (160°C).
2. In a small bowl, mix together the brown sugar and ground cinnamon. Set this cinnamon sugar mixture aside.
3. Unroll the puff pastry sheet on its paper and brush the entire surface with the melted butter.
4. Sprinkle the cinnamon sugar mixture evenly over the buttered pastry sheet.
5. Roll up the pastry sheet tightly, creating a log. Make sure the seam is sealed.
6. Cut the rolled pastry into 1-inch wide slices to form cinnamon rolls.
7. Place the cinnamon rolls with the spiral side facing up into a greased baking pan.
8. Carefully transfer the baking pan with the cinnamon rolls into the air fryer basket.
9. Air-fry the cinnamon rolls at 320°F for approximately 18-20 minutes, or until they are golden brown and cooked through.
10. Once the cinnamon rolls are done, remove them from the air fryer and allow them to cool for 5-10 minutes.
11. While the cinnamon rolls are cooling, prepare the icing. In a small bowl, combine the softened mascarpone cheese, vanilla extract, and salt. Whisk until the mixture is smooth and creamy.
12. Gradually add confectioners' sugar to the mascarpone mixture, continuing to whisk until fully blended.
13. To achieve the desired consistency for your icing, slowly add milk, one teaspoon at a time, until the glaze is pourable but still has some thickness.
14. Drizzle the icing over the warm cinnamon rolls while they are still in the baking pan.
15. Scatter lemon zest over the top of the cinnamon rolls to add a zesty twist.
16. Serve the Mascarpone Iced Cinnamon Rolls while they are still warm and enjoy!

Crunchy French Toast Sticks

Servings: 2
Cooking Time: 9 Minutes
Ingredients:
- 2 eggs, beaten
- 180 ml milk
- 1/2 teaspoon vanilla extract
- 1/2 teaspoon ground cinnamon
- 120 grams crushed crunchy cinnamon cereal or any cereal flakes
- 4 slices of thick bread (e.g., Texas Toast or other bread that you can slice into 2.5 cm thick slices)
- Maple syrup, for serving
- Vegetable oil or melted butter for greasing

Directions:

1. In a shallow bowl, combine the beaten eggs, milk, vanilla extract, and ground cinnamon.
2. Place the crushed cereal in a second shallow bowl.
3. Trim the crusts off the slices of bread and cut each slice into 3 sticks.
4. Dip the sticks of bread into the egg mixture, turning them over to coat all sides. Allow the bread sticks to absorb the egg mixture for about ten seconds, but don't let them get too wet.
5. Roll the bread sticks in the cereal crumbs, pressing the cereal gently onto all sides to make sure it adheres to the bread.
6. Preheat the air fryer to 200°C (400°F).
7. Spray or brush the air fryer basket with oil or melted butter.
8. Place the coated sticks in the basket, and it's okay to stack a few on top of each other in the opposite direction.
9. Air-fry for 9 minutes, turning the sticks over a couple of times during the cooking process to ensure even crisping.
10. Serve the warm Crunchy French Toast Sticks with maple syrup or some berries.

Broccoli Cornbread

Servings: 6
Cooking Time: 18 Minutes
Ingredients:
- 240ml frozen chopped broccoli, thawed and drained
- 60ml cottage cheese
- 1 egg, beaten
- 30ml minced onion
- 30ml melted butter
- 120ml flour
- 120ml yellow cornmeal
- 5ml baking powder
- 2.5ml salt
- 60ml milk, plus 30ml (2 tablespoons)
- Cooking spray

Directions:
1. Place the thawed broccoli in a colander and press it with a spoon to squeeze out excess moisture.
2. In a large bowl, stir together all the ingredients.
3. Spray a 15 x 15 cm (6 x 6-inch) baking pan with cooking spray.
4. Spread the batter in the pan and cook in the air fryer at 165°C (330°F) for 18 minutes or until the cornbread is lightly browned and starts to pull away from the sides of the pan.
5. Enjoy your Broccoli Cornbread!

Apricot-cheese Mini Pies

Servings: 6
Cooking Time: 35 Minutes
Ingredients:
- 2 refrigerated pie crusts
- 80 milliliters (1/3 cup) apricot preserves
- 5 milliliters (1 teaspoon) cornstarch
- 120 milliliters (1/2 cup) vanilla yogurt
- 28 grams (1 ounce) cream cheese
- 5 milliliters (1 teaspoon) sugar
- Rainbow sprinkles

Directions:
1. Preheat your air fryer to 190°C (370°F).
2. Lay out the pie crusts on a flat surface. Cut each sheet of pie crust into three rectangles, giving you a total of 6 rectangles.
3. In a small bowl, mix the apricot preserves and cornstarch.
4. Cover the top half of one rectangle with 15 milliliters (1 tablespoon) of the preserve mixture. Repeat this step for all rectangles.
5. Fold the bottom half of the crust over the preserve-covered top half, creating a rectangle. Crimp and seal all the edges with a fork.
6. Lightly coat each tart with cooking oil, ensuring they are not stacked on top of each other.
7. Place the tarts into the air fryer and bake for 10 minutes.
8. While the tarts are baking, prepare the frosting by mixing the vanilla yogurt, cream cheese, and sugar until well combined.
9. Once the tarts are done, allow them to cool completely in the air fryer.
10. Frost the cooled tarts with the yogurt and cream cheese mixture.
11. Top the frosted tarts with rainbow sprinkles for a delightful touch.
12. Serve your delicious apricot-cheese mini pies.

Green Onion Pancakes

Servings: 4
Cooking Time: 8 Minutes
Ingredients:
- 250 grams all-purpose flour
- 2.5 grams salt
- 180 ml hot water
- 15 ml vegetable oil
- 15 ml butter, melted
- 160 grams finely chopped green onions

- 15 ml black sesame seeds, for garnish

Directions:

1. In a large bowl, whisk together the flour and salt. Make a well in the center and pour in the hot water. Quickly stir the flour mixture together until a dough forms. Knead the dough for 5 minutes; then cover with a warm, wet towel and set aside for 30 minutes to rest.
2. In a small bowl, mix together the vegetable oil and melted butter.
3. On a floured surface, place the dough and cut it into 8 pieces. Working with 1 piece of dough at a time, use a rolling pin to roll out the dough until it's ¼ inch thick; then brush the surface with the oil and butter mixture and sprinkle with green onions. Next, fold the dough in half and then in half again. Roll out the dough again until it's ¼ inch thick and brush with the oil and butter mixture and green onions. Fold the dough in half and then in half again and roll out one last time until it's ¼ inch thick. Repeat this technique with all 8 pieces.
4. Meanwhile, preheat the air fryer to 200°C (400°F).
5. Place 1 or 2 pancakes into the air fryer basket (or as many as will fit in your fryer), and cook for 2 minutes or until crispy and golden brown. Repeat until all the pancakes are cooked.
6. Top with black sesame seeds for garnish, if desired.
7. Serve and enjoy your Green Onion Pancakes with the UK units provided in the recipe!

Goat Cheese, Beet, And Kale Frittata

Servings: 6
Cooking Time: 20 Minutes

Ingredients:

- 6 large eggs
- 2.5 ml garlic powder
- 1.25 ml black pepper
- 1.25 ml salt
- 240 ml chopped kale
- 240 ml cooked and chopped red beets
- 80 ml crumbled goat cheese

Directions:

1. Preheat the air fryer to 160°C (320°F).
2. In a medium bowl, whisk the eggs with the garlic powder, black pepper, and salt. Mix in the chopped kale, red beets, and crumbled goat cheese.
3. Spray an oven-safe 7-inch springform pan with cooking spray. Pour the egg mixture into the pan and place it in the air fryer basket.
4. Cook for 20 minutes, or until the internal temperature reaches 63°C (145°F).
5. When the frittata is cooked, let it set for 5 minutes before removing it from the pan.
6. Slice and serve immediately.

Ham And Cheddar Gritters

Servings: 6
Cooking Time: 12 Minutes

Ingredients:

- 950 ml water
- 190 g quick-cooking grits
- 1/4 teaspoon salt
- 30 g butter
- 190 g grated Cheddar cheese, divided
- 140 g finely diced ham
- 15 g chopped chives
- Salt and freshly ground black pepper
- 1 egg, beaten
- 160 g panko breadcrumbs
- Vegetable oil

Directions:

1. Bring the water to a boil in a saucepan. Whisk in the grits and 1/4 teaspoon of salt, and cook for 7 minutes until the grits are soft. Remove the pan from the heat and stir in the butter and 140 g of the grated Cheddar cheese. Transfer the grits to a bowl and let them cool for just 10 to 15 minutes.
2. Stir the ham, chives, and the rest of the cheese into the grits and season with salt and pepper to taste. Add the beaten egg and refrigerate the mixture for 30 minutes. (Try not to chill the grits much longer than 30 minutes, or the mixture will be too firm to shape into patties.)
3. While the grit mixture is chilling, make the country gravy and set it aside.
4. Place the panko breadcrumbs in a shallow dish. Measure out 1/4-cup portions of the grits mixture and shape them into patties. Coat all sides of the patties with the panko breadcrumbs, patting them with your hands so the crumbs adhere to the patties. You should have about 16 patties. Spray both sides of the patties with oil.
5. Preheat the air fryer to 200°C (400°F).
6. In batches of 5 or 6, air-fry the fritters for 8 minutes. Using a flat spatula, flip the fritters over and air-fry for another 4 minutes.
7. Serve hot with country gravy.

Avocado Toasts With Poached Eggs

Servings: 4
Cooking Time: 15 Minutes
Ingredients:
- 4 eggs
- Salt and pepper to taste
- 4 slices of bread, toasted
- 1 pitted avocado, sliced
- 1/2 tsp chili powder
- 1/2 tsp dried rosemary

Directions:
1. Preheat your air fryer to 160°C (320°F).
2. Grease four ramekins and carefully crack one egg into each. Season with a pinch of salt and black pepper.
3. Place the greased ramekins into the air fryer basket and bake for 6-8 minutes until the eggs are poached to your desired level of doneness.
4. While the eggs are cooking, prepare the avocado topping. Scoop the flesh of the avocado into a small bowl and season it with salt, black pepper, chili powder, and dried rosemary. Use a fork to lightly smash the avocado, creating a spreadable consistency.
5. Once the eggs are done, remove them from the air fryer.
6. Spread the smashed avocado evenly over the toasted bread slices.
7. Gently spoon one poached egg onto each slice of avocado toast.
8. Season with additional salt and pepper if desired.
9. Serve your delicious avocado toasts with poached eggs immediately and enjoy!

Garlic Bread Knots

Servings: 8
Cooking Time: 5 Minutes
Ingredients:
- 60 ml melted butter
- 10 ml garlic powder
- 5 ml dried parsley
- 1 (312-gram) tube of refrigerated French bread dough

Directions:
1. Mix the melted butter, garlic powder, and dried parsley in a small bowl and set it aside.
2. To make smaller knots, cut the long tube of bread dough into 16 slices. If you want to make bigger knots, slice the dough into 8 slices.
3. Shape each slice into a long rope about 15 cm (6 inches) long by rolling it on a flat surface with the palm of your hands.
4. Tie each rope into a knot and place them on a plate.
5. Preheat the air fryer to 175°C (350°F).
6. Transfer half of the bread knots into the air fryer basket, leaving space between each knot.
7. Brush each knot with the butter mixture using a pastry brush.
8. Air-fry for 5 minutes.
9. Remove the baked knots and brush a little more of the garlic butter mixture on each.
10. Repeat with the remaining bread knots and serve them warm.

Garlic-cheese Biscuits

Servings: 8
Cooking Time: 8 Minutes
Ingredients:
- 125 grams self-raising flour
- 5 ml garlic powder
- 30 grams butter, diced
- 56 grams sharp Cheddar cheese, grated
- 120 ml milk
- Cooking spray

Directions:
1. Preheat the air fryer to 165°C (330°F).
2. Combine self-raising flour and garlic powder in a medium bowl and stir together.
3. Using a pastry blender or knives, cut the diced butter into the dry ingredients.
4. Stir in the grated cheese.
5. Add milk and stir until a stiff dough forms. If the dough is too sticky to handle, stir in 1 or 2 more tablespoons of self-raising flour before shaping. The biscuits should be firm enough to hold their shape; otherwise, they may stick to the air fryer basket.
6. Divide the dough into 8 portions and shape them into 5 cm (2-inch) biscuits about 2 cm (¾-inch) thick.
7. Spray the air fryer basket with nonstick cooking spray.
8. Place all 8 biscuits in the basket and cook at 165°C (330°F) for 8 minutes.

Egg & Bacon Pockets

Servings: 4
Cooking Time: 50 Minutes
Ingredients:
- 30 ml olive oil
- 4 bacon slices, chopped
- 1/4 red bell pepper, diced
- 80 ml scallions, chopped
- 4 eggs, beaten
- 80 ml grated Swiss cheese

- 125 grams flour
- 7.5 grams baking powder
- 2.5 grams salt
- 240 ml Greek yogurt
- 1 egg white, beaten
- 10 ml Italian seasoning
- 15 ml Tabasco sauce

Directions:
1. Warm the olive oil in a skillet over medium heat and add the chopped bacon. Stir-fry for 3-4 minutes or until it becomes crispy.
2. Add the diced red bell pepper and chopped scallions to the skillet and sauté for another 3-4 minutes.
3. Pour in the beaten eggs and stir-fry to scramble them for about 3 minutes. Stir in the grated Swiss cheese and set aside to cool.
4. Sift the flour, baking powder, and salt into a bowl. Add the Greek yogurt and mix together until well combined.
5. Transfer the dough to a floured workspace and knead it for 3 minutes or until it becomes smooth.
6. Divide the dough into 4 equal balls and roll out each ball into a round disc.
7. Divide the bacon-egg mixture equally between the rounds.
8. Fold the dough over the filling and seal the edges with a fork.
9. Brush the pockets with beaten egg white and sprinkle them with Italian seasoning.
10. Preheat the air fryer to 180°C (350°F).
11. Arrange the pockets on the greased frying basket in a single layer.
12. Bake for 9-11 minutes, flipping them once, until they turn golden.
13. Serve your Egg & Bacon Pockets with Tabasco sauce.

Breakfast Frittata

Servings: 2
Cooking Time: 25 Minutes

Ingredients:
- 4 cooked pancetta slices, chopped
- 5 eggs
- Salt and pepper to taste
- 1/2 leek, thinly sliced
- 120g grated cheddar cheese
- 1 tomato, sliced
- 30g iceberg lettuce, torn
- 30ml milk

Directions:
1. Preheat your air fryer to 160°C (320°F).
2. In a bowl, beat the eggs, milk, salt, and pepper.
3. Mix in the chopped pancetta and grated cheddar cheese.
4. Transfer the mixture to a baking pan greased with olive oil.
5. Top the mixture with tomato slices and thinly sliced leek.
6. Place the baking pan in the air fryer basket.
7. Bake for 14 minutes in the air fryer.
8. Allow the frittata to cool for 5 minutes.
9. Serve your delicious Breakfast Frittata with torn iceberg lettuce.
10. Enjoy your meal!

Chocolate Almond Crescent Rolls

Servings: 4
Cooking Time: 8 Minutes

Ingredients:
- 1 (226g) tube of crescent roll dough
- 150g semi-sweet or bittersweet chocolate chunks
- 1 egg white, lightly beaten
- 30g sliced almonds
- Powdered sugar, for dusting
- Butter or oil

Directions:
1. Preheat the air fryer to 175°C (350°F).
2. Unwrap the crescent roll dough and separate it into triangles with the points facing away from you. Place a row of chocolate chunks along the bottom edge of the dough. (If you are using chips, make it a double row.) Roll the dough up around the chocolate and then place another row of chunks on the dough. Roll again and finish with one or two chocolate chunks. Be sure to leave the end free of chocolate so that it can adhere to the rest of the roll.
3. Brush the tops of the crescent rolls with the lightly beaten egg white and sprinkle the almonds on top, pressing them into the crescent dough so they adhere.
4. Brush the bottom of the air fryer basket with butter or oil and transfer the crescent rolls to the basket.
5. Air-fry at 175°C (350°F) for 8 minutes.
6. Remove and let the crescent rolls cool before dusting with powdered sugar and serving.

Crunchy Granola Muffins

Servings: 4
Cooking Time: 15 Minutes

Ingredients:
- 120 grams walnut pieces
- 120 grams sunflower seeds
- 120 grams coconut flakes

- 55 grams granulated sugar
- 15 grams coconut flour
- 15 grams pecan flour
- 2 tsp ground cinnamon
- 30 ml melted butter
- 30 ml almond butter
- 1/8 tsp salt

Directions:
1. Preheat the air fryer to 150°C (300°F).
2. In a bowl, mix together the walnut pieces, sunflower seeds, coconut flakes, granulated sugar, coconut flour, pecan flour, ground cinnamon, melted butter, almond butter, and salt.
3. Spoon the mixture into an ungreased round 4-cup baking dish.
4. Place the baking dish in the air fryer basket.
5. Bake for 6 minutes, stirring once during the cooking process to ensure even browning.
6. Remove the granola mixture from the air fryer and transfer it to an airtight container.
7. Allow it to cool for 10 minutes, then cover and store at room temperature until ready to serve.

Blueberry Pannenkoek (dutch Pancake)

Servings: 4
Cooking Time: 30 Minutes
Ingredients:
- 3 eggs, beaten
- 120g buckwheat flour
- 120ml milk
- 2.5ml vanilla extract
- 360g blueberries, crushed
- 30g powdered sugar

Directions:
1. Preheat your air fryer to 165°C (330°F).
2. In a bowl, mix together the beaten eggs, buckwheat flour, milk, and vanilla extract until well combined.
3. Pour the batter into a greased baking pan and place it in the air fryer.
4. Bake until the pancake is puffed and golden, which should take about 12-16 minutes.
5. Remove the pan from the air fryer and carefully flip the pancake onto a plate.
6. Top the pancake with crushed blueberries and sprinkle powdered sugar over it.
7. Serve your delicious Blueberry Pannenkoek (Dutch Pancake) immediately.
8. Enjoy!

Apple French Toast Sandwich

Servings: 1
Cooking Time: 30 Minutes
Ingredients:
- 2 slices of white bread
- 2 eggs
- 5 milliliters (1 teaspoon) cinnamon
- 1/2 apple, peeled and sliced
- 15 grams (1 tablespoon) brown sugar
- 60 milliliters (1/4 cup) whipped cream

Directions:
1. Preheat your air fryer to 180°C (350°F).
2. In a small bowl, coat the sliced apple with brown sugar.
3. In a separate bowl, whisk the eggs and cinnamon together until they are fluffy and well blended.
4. Dip the bread slices into the egg mixture, ensuring they are evenly coated.
5. Grease the air fryer basket or rack, and place the coated bread slices in it.
6. Top the bread slices with the apple slices.
7. Air fry for approximately 20 minutes, flipping the sandwich once during cooking. Continue cooking until the bread is nicely browned, and the apples become crispy.
8. Remove one French toast slice from the air fryer and place it on a serving plate.
9. Spoon the whipped cream onto the toast and spread it evenly.
10. Scoop the caramelized apple slices onto the whipped cream-covered toast.
11. Top with the second slice of French toast to create a sandwich.
12. Serve your delightful apple French toast sandwich immediately and enjoy!

Appetizers And Snacks Recipes

Chili Pepper Popcorn

Servings: 18
Cooking Time: 5 Minutes
Ingredients:
- 225 grams jalapeño peppers
- 30 grams cornstarch
- 1 egg
- 15 ml lime juice
- 30 grams plain breadcrumbs
- 30 grams panko breadcrumbs
- 2.5 grams salt
- Oil for misting or cooking spray
- Filling:
- 115 grams cream cheese
- 1 teaspoon grated lime zest
- 0.25 teaspoon chile powder
- 0.125 teaspoon garlic powder
- 0.25 teaspoon salt
- Instructions:
- In a small bowl, combine all the filling ingredients (cream cheese, grated lime zest, chile powder, garlic powder, and salt). Mix well and refrigerate the filling while you prepare the peppers.
- Cut the jalapeño peppers into 1.25 cm (1/2-inch) lengthwise slices. Use a small, sharp knife to remove the seeds and veins.
- For milder appetizers, discard the seeds and veins.
- For spicier appetizers, finely chop some of the seeds and veins and stir them into the filling, adding gradually until the filling reaches your desired level of heat.
- Stuff each pepper slice with the prepared filling.
- Place the cornstarch in a shallow dish.
- In another shallow dish, beat together the egg and lime juice.
- In a third shallow dish, combine the plain breadcrumbs, panko breadcrumbs, and salt. Mix well.
- Dip each pepper slice first into the cornstarch, shaking off excess, then dip it into the egg mixture.
- Roll the pepper slice in the breadcrumb mixture, pressing to make the coating stick.
- Place the coated pepper slices on a plate in a single layer and freeze them for 30 minutes.
- Preheat your air fryer to 200°C (390°F).
- Spray the frozen peppers with oil or cooking spray to lightly coat them.
- Arrange the pepper slices in a single layer in the air fryer basket and cook for 5 minutes, or until they are crispy and golden brown.

Corn Dog Bites

Servings: 3
Cooking Time: 12 Minutes
Ingredients:
- 240g Purchased cornbread stuffing mix
- 40g All-purpose flour
- 2 Large eggs, well beaten
- 3 Hot dogs, cut into 5cm pieces (vegetarian hot dogs, if preferred)
- Vegetable oil spray

Directions:
1. Preheat the air fryer to 190°C (375°F).
2. Put the cornbread stuffing mix in a food processor. Cover and pulse to grind into a mixture like fine bread crumbs.
3. Set up and fill three shallow soup plates or small pie plates on your counter: one for the flour, one for the beaten eggs, and one for the stuffing mix crumbs.
4. Dip a hot dog piece in the flour to coat it completely, then gently shake off any excess. Dip the hot dog piece into the beaten eggs and gently roll it around to coat all surfaces. Set the hot dog piece in the stuffing mix crumbs and roll it gently to coat it evenly and well on all sides, including the ends. Set it aside on a cutting board and continue dipping and coating the remaining hot dog pieces.
5. Give the coated hot dog pieces a generous coating of vegetable oil spray on all sides, then set them in the basket in one layer with some space between them.
6. Air-fry undisturbed for 10 minutes, or until golden brown and crunchy. (You may need to add 2 minutes in the air fryer if the temperature is at 180°C.)
7. Use a nonstick-safe spatula, and perhaps a flatware fork for balance, to transfer the corn dog bites to a wire rack. Cool for 5 minutes before serving.

Chicken Nachos

Servings: 6
Cooking Time: 25 Minutes
Ingredients:
- 55g baked corn tortilla chips
- 225g leftover roast chicken, shredded
- 120g canned black beans
- 1 red bell pepper, chopped
- 30g grated carrot
- 1 jalapeño pepper, minced
- 75g grated Swiss cheese
- 1 tomato, chopped

Directions:
1. Preheat the air fryer to 180°C (360°F).
2. Lay the tortilla chips in a single layer in a baking pan or the air fryer basket.
3. Add the shredded chicken, black beans, chopped red bell pepper, grated carrot, minced jalapeño, and grated Swiss cheese on top of the tortilla chips.
4. Bake in the air fryer for 9-12 minutes, making sure the cheese melts and becomes slightly browned.
5. Serve the Chicken Nachos garnished with chopped tomatoes.

Bacon & Blue Cheese Tartlets

Servings: 6
Cooking Time: 30 Minutes
Ingredients:
- 6 bacon rashers
- 16 phyllo tartlet shells
- 120 grams diced blue cheese
- 45 ml apple jelly

Directions:
1. Preheat the air fryer to 200°C (400°F).
2. Place the bacon rashers in a single layer in the air fryer basket. Air Fry for 14 minutes, turning them once halfway through. Remove the cooked bacon and drain it on paper towels. Once it has cooled, crumble the bacon into small pieces.
3. Wipe the air fryer clean after cooking the bacon.
4. Fill the tartlet shells with the crumbled bacon and the diced blue cheese. Add a small dab of apple jelly on top of the filling.
5. Lower the air fryer temperature to 180°C (350°F) and place the filled tartlet shells in the frying basket.
6. Air Fry until the cheese melts and the tartlet shells turn brown, which should take about 5-6 minutes.
7. Remove the tartlets from the air fryer and serve.

Cholula Avocado Fries

Servings: 2
Cooking Time: 20 Minutes
Ingredients:
- 1 egg, beaten
- 30g flour
- 10g ground flaxseed
- 1.25ml Cholula sauce
- Salt to taste
- 1 avocado, cut into fries

Directions:
1. Preheat the air fryer to 190°C (375°F).
2. Mix the beaten egg and Cholula sauce in a bowl.
3. In another bowl, combine the remaining ingredients, except for the avocado.
4. Submerge the avocado slices in the egg mixture and dredge them into the flour mixture to coat evenly.
5. Place the avocado fries in the lightly greased air fryer basket.
6. Air fry for 5 minutes or until they are golden and crispy.
7. Serve your Cholula Avocado Fries immediately.

Homemade French Fries

Servings: 2
Cooking Time: 25 Minutes
Ingredients:
- 2 to 3 russet potatoes, peeled and cut into 1.3 cm (1/2-inch) sticks
- 10 to 15 ml (2 to 3 teaspoons) olive or vegetable oil
- Salt

Directions:
1. Bring a large saucepan of salted water to a boil on the stovetop while you peel and cut the potatoes.
2. Blanch the potatoes in the boiling salted water for 4 minutes. Meanwhile, Preheat the air fryer to 204°C (400°F).
3. Strain the potatoes and rinse them with cold water. Dry them well with a clean kitchen towel.
4. Toss the dried potato sticks gently with the oil to coat them evenly.
5. Place the potato sticks in the air fryer basket.
6. Air-fry for 25 minutes, shaking the basket a few times while the fries cook to help them brown evenly.
7. Season the fries with salt halfway through cooking.
8. Serve the fries warm with your choice of condiments, such as tomato ketchup, Sriracha mayonnaise, or a mix of lemon zest, Parmesan cheese, and parsley.

Artichoke Samosas

Servings: 6
Cooking Time: 25 Minutes
Ingredients:
- 125 grams minced artichoke hearts
- 60 grams ricotta cheese
- 1 egg white
- 3 tablespoons grated mozzarella
- ½ teaspoon dried thyme
- 6 sheets of filo pastry
- 2 tablespoons melted butter
- 240 ml mango chutney

Directions:
1. Preheat the air frycr to 200°C (400°F).
2. In a small bowl, mix together the ricotta cheese, egg white, minced artichoke hearts, grated mozzarella cheese, and dried thyme until well blended.
3. When you take out the filo pastry sheets, cover them with a damp kitchen towel to prevent them from drying out while you work with them.
4. Take one sheet of filo pastry and place it on the work surface. Cut it into thirds lengthwise.
5. At the base of each strip, place about 1 ½ teaspoons of the filling.
6. Fold the bottom right-hand corner of the strip over to the left-hand side to create a triangle. Continue folding and forming triangles along the strip.
7. Brush the triangle with melted butter to seal the edges.
8. Place the prepared triangles in the greased frying basket of the air fryer.
9. Bake until the samosas are golden and crisp, which should take approximately 4 minutes.
10. Serve the Artichoke Samosas with mango chutney.

Fried Pickles With Homemade Ranch

Servings: 8
Cooking Time: 8 Minutes
Ingredients:
- 120 grams all-purpose flour
- 2 teaspoons dried dill
- 0.5 teaspoon paprika
- 180 ml buttermilk
- 1 egg
- 4 large kosher dill pickles, sliced 0.6 cm (¼-inch) thick
- 200 grams panko breadcrumbs
- Cooking spray

Directions:
1. Preheat your air fryer to 190°C (380°F).
2. In a medium bowl, whisk together the all-purpose flour, dried dill, paprika, buttermilk, and egg until you have a smooth batter.
3. Dip the thick slices of dill pickles into the batter, ensuring they are well coated.
4. Next, dredge the coated pickles in the panko breadcrumbs, pressing gently to adhere the breadcrumbs to the pickles.
5. Place a single layer of breaded pickle slices into the air fryer basket. Spray the pickles with cooking spray.
6. Cook for 4 minutes, then carefully turn them over, and cook for another 4 minutes or until they are golden brown and crispy.
7. Repeat this process until all the pickle chips have been cooked.
8. Serve your "Fried" Pickles with Homemade Ranch or your favorite dipping sauce.

Chili Black Bean Empanadas

Servings: 4
Cooking Time: 20 Minutes
Ingredients:
- 120g cooked black beans
- 60g white onions, diced
- 5g red chili powder
- 2.5g paprika
- 2.5g garlic salt
- 2.5g ground cumin
- 2.5g ground cinnamon
- 4 empanada dough shells

Directions:
1. Preheat the air fryer to 180°C (350°F).
2. Stir-fry black beans and onions in a pan over medium heat for 5 minutes. Add chili powder, paprika, garlic salt, ground cumin, and ground cinnamon. Set aside, covered, when the onions are soft, and the beans are hot.
3. On a clean workspace, lay out the empanada shells. Spoon the bean mixture onto the shells without spilling.
4. Fold the shells over to cover fully and seal the edges with water. Press the edges with a fork to ensure they are sealed.
5. Transfer the empanadas to the foil-lined frying basket and bake for 15 minutes, flipping them once halfway through cooking, or until they are golden.
6. Serve your Chili Black Bean Empanadas.

Antipasto-stuffed Cherry Tomatoes

Servings: 12
Cooking Time: 9 Minutes
Ingredients:
- 12 Large cherry tomatoes, preferably Campari tomatoes (about 42.5 grams each and the size of golf balls)
- 65 grams Seasoned Italian-style dried bread crumbs (gluten-free, if a concern)
- 20 grams Finely grated Parmesan cheese
- 40 grams Finely chopped pitted black olives
- 40 grams Finely chopped marinated artichoke hearts
- 30 ml Marinade from the artichokes
- 4 Sun-dried tomatoes (dry, not packed in oil), finely chopped
- Olive oil spray

Directions:
1. Preheat the air fryer to 200°C (400°F).
2. Cut the top off each fresh tomato, exposing the seeds and pulp. (The tops can be saved for a snack, sprinkled with some kosher salt, to tide you over while the stuffed tomatoes cook.) Cut a very small slice off the bottom of each tomato (no cutting into the pulp) so it will stand up flat on your work surface. Use a melon baller to remove and discard the seeds and pulp from each tomato.
3. In a bowl, mix the bread crumbs, cheese, olives, artichoke hearts, marinade, and sun-dried tomatoes until well combined. Stuff this mixture into each prepared tomato, about 1½ tablespoons in each. Generously coat the tops of the tomatoes with olive oil spray.
4. Set the tomatoes stuffing side up in the basket. Air-fry undisturbed for 9 minutes, or until the stuffing has browned a bit and the tomatoes are blistered in places.
5. Remove the basket and cool the tomatoes in it for 5 minutes. Then use kitchen tongs to gently transfer the tomatoes to a serving platter.

Classic Chicken Wings

Servings: 8
Cooking Time: 20 Minutes
Ingredients:
- 16 chicken wings
- 30g all-purpose flour
- 0.25g garlic powder
- 0.25g paprika
- 1g salt
- 1g black pepper
- 60g butter
- 120ml hot sauce
- 2.5ml Worcestershire sauce
- 57g crumbled blue cheese, for garnish

Directions:
1. Preheat the air fryer to 193°C (380°F).
2. Pat the chicken wings dry with paper towels.
3. In a medium bowl, mix together the flour, garlic powder, paprika, salt, and pepper.
4. Toss the chicken wings with the flour mixture, dusting off any excess.
5. Place the chicken wings in the air fryer basket, making sure that the chicken wings aren't touching.
6. Cook the chicken wings for 10 minutes, turn them over, and cook for another 5 minutes.
7. Raise the temperature to 204°C (400°F) and continue crisping the chicken wings for an additional 3 to 5 minutes.
8. Meanwhile, in a microwave-safe bowl, melt the butter and hot sauce for 1 to 2 minutes in the microwave. Remove from the microwave and stir in the Worcestershire sauce.
9. When the chicken wings have cooked, immediately transfer the chicken wings into the hot sauce mixture.
10. Serve the coated chicken wings on a plate, and top with crumbled blue cheese.

Cheese Arancini

Servings: 8
Cooking Time: 12 Minutes
Ingredients:
- 240ml Water
- 120g Raw white Arborio rice
- 7.5g Butter
- 1/4 teaspoon Table salt
- 8 ¾-inch semi-firm mozzarella cubes (not fresh mozzarella)
- 2 Large eggs, well beaten
- 120g Seasoned Italian-style dried bread crumbs (gluten-free, if needed)
- Olive oil spray

Directions:
1. Combine the water, rice, butter, and salt in a small saucepan. Bring to a boil over medium-high heat, stirring occasionally. Cover, reduce the heat to very low, and simmer very slowly for 20 minutes.
2. Remove the saucepan from the heat and let it stand, covered, for 10 minutes. Uncover it and fluff the rice. Cool it for 20 minutes. (The rice can be made up to 1 hour in advance; keep it covered in its saucepan.)
3. Preheat the air fryer to 190°C (375°F).

4. Set up and fill two shallow soup plates or small bowls on your counter: one with the beaten eggs and one with the bread crumbs.

5. With clean but wet hands, scoop up about 2 tablespoons of the cooked rice and form it into a ball. Push a cube of mozzarella into the middle of the ball and seal the cheese inside.

6. Dip the ball in the beaten eggs to coat it completely, letting any excess egg drip back into the bowl. Roll the ball in the bread crumbs to coat it evenly but lightly. Set it aside and continue making more rice balls.

7. Generously spray the rice balls with olive oil spray and place them in the air fryer basket in a single layer, ensuring they do not touch.

8. Air-fry the rice balls undisturbed for 10 minutes, or until they are crunchy and golden brown. If the air fryer temperature is set to 180°C (360°F), you may need to add 2 minutes to the cooking time.

9. Use a nonstick-safe spatula, and possibly a flatware spoon for balance, to gently transfer the rice balls to a wire rack.

10. Cool the Cheese Arancini for at least 5 minutes or up to 20 minutes before serving.

Chili Corn On The Cob

Servings: 4
Cooking Time: 30 Minutes
Ingredients:
- Salt and pepper to taste
- 2.5g smoked paprika
- 1.25g chili powder
- 4 ears of corn, halved
- 15g butter, melted
- 60ml lime juice
- 2.5g lime zest
- 1 lime, quartered

Directions:
1. Preheat the air fryer to 200°C (400°F).
2. Combine salt, pepper, lime juice, lime zest, paprika, and chili powder in a small bowl.
3. Toss the corn and melted butter in a large bowl, then add the seasonings from the small bowl. Toss until the corn is well coated.
4. Arrange the corn in a single layer in the frying basket.
5. Air fry for 10 minutes, then turn the corn.
6. Air fry for another 8 minutes or until the corn is tender and slightly charred.
7. Squeeze lime juice over the corn and serve with lime quarters.

Cauliflower "tater" Tots

Servings: 6
Cooking Time: 10 Minutes
Ingredients:
- 1 head of cauliflower
- 2 eggs
- 30g all-purpose flour*
- 125g grated Parmesan cheese
- 1 teaspoon salt
- Freshly ground black pepper
- Vegetable or olive oil, in a spray bottle

Directions:
1. Grate the head of cauliflower with a box grater or finely chop it in a food processor. You should have about 875ml (3½ cups) of grated cauliflower.
2. Place the chopped cauliflower in the center of a clean kitchen towel and twist the towel tightly to squeeze all the water out of the cauliflower. You may need to do this in two batches to ensure all the water is removed.
3. Transfer the squeezed cauliflower to a large bowl. Add the eggs, all-purpose flour, grated Parmesan cheese, salt, and freshly ground black pepper. Mix well until all the ingredients are combined.
4. Shape the cauliflower mixture into small cylinders or "tater tot" shapes, rolling roughly one tablespoon of the mixture at a time. Place the tots on a cookie sheet lined with paper towels to absorb any residual moisture.
5. Spray the cauliflower tots all over with vegetable or olive oil using an oil spray bottle.
6. Preheat the air fryer to 200°C (400°F).
7. Air-fry the tots at 200°C (400°F), in a single layer, for 10 minutes, turning them over for the last few minutes of the cooking process to ensure even browning.
8. Season the cauliflower tots with salt and black pepper to taste.
9. Serve the "Tater" Tots hot with your favorite dipping sauce.

Beef Steak Sliders

Servings: 8
Cooking Time: 22 Minutes
Ingredients:
- 450 grams top sirloin steaks, about 2 cm thick
- Salt and pepper
- 2 large onions, thinly sliced
- 15 ml extra-light olive oil
- 8 slider buns
- Horseradish Mayonnaise:
- 240 ml light mayonnaise

- 20 ml prepared horseradish
- 10 ml Worcestershire sauce
- 5 ml coarse brown mustard

Directions:

1. Place the steak in the air fryer basket and cook at 200°C for 6 minutes. Turn and cook for an additional 6 minutes for medium-rare. If you prefer your steak medium, continue cooking for 3 minutes.
2. While the steak is cooking, prepare the Horseradish Mayonnaise by mixing all the ingredients together.
3. When the steak is cooked, remove it from the air fryer, sprinkle with salt and pepper to taste, and set it aside to rest.
4. Toss the onion slices with the oil and place them in the air fryer basket. Cook at 200°C for 7 minutes, until the onion rings are soft and browned.
5. Slice the steak into very thin slices.
6. Spread the slider buns with the horseradish mayo and pile on the meat and onions. Serve with the remaining horseradish dressing for dipping.

Avocado Toast With Lemony Shrimp

Servings: 4
Cooking Time: 6 Minutes

Ingredients:

- 170 grams Raw medium shrimp (30 to 35 per pound), peeled and deveined
- 7.5 ml Finely grated lemon zest
- 10 ml Lemon juice
- 7.5 ml Minced garlic
- 7.5 ml Ground black pepper
- 4 slices of rye or whole-wheat bread (gluten-free, if needed)
- 2 Ripe Hass avocados, halved, pitted, peeled, and roughly chopped
- Coarse sea salt or kosher salt for garnishing

Directions:

1. Preheat the air fryer to 200°C (400°F).
2. Toss the shrimp, lemon zest, lemon juice, garlic, and black pepper in a bowl until the shrimp are evenly coated.
3. Once the air fryer reaches the desired temperature, use kitchen tongs to place the shrimp in a single layer in the basket. Air-fry them undisturbed for 4 minutes, or until the shrimp turn pink and are barely firm. Use kitchen tongs to transfer the cooked shrimp to a cutting board.
4. In batches, place as many slices of bread as will fit in the air fryer basket in one layer. Air-fry them undisturbed for 2 minutes, just until they are warmed through and crisp. The bread will not brown much.
5. Arrange the toasted bread slices on a clean, dry work surface. Divide the chopped avocado among them and gently smash the avocado into a coarse paste using the tines of a fork.
6. Top the avocado toasts with the cooked shrimp and sprinkle with salt as a garnish.

Asian Five-spice Wings

Servings: 4
Cooking Time: 15 Minutes

Ingredients:

- 907 grams chicken wings
- 120 ml Asian-style salad dressing
- 30 ml Chinese five-spice powder

Directions:

1. Begin by cutting off the wing tips and discard them or save them for making stock. Then, cut the remaining wing pieces in two at the joint.
2. Place the wing pieces in a large sealable plastic bag. Pour in the Asian dressing, seal the bag, and massage the marinade into the wings until they are well coated. Refrigerate for at least an hour to marinate.
3. After marinating, remove the wings from the bag, drain off any excess marinade, and place the wings in the air fryer basket.
4. Cook the wings at 180°C (360°F) for 15 minutes or until the juices run clear. About halfway through the cooking time, shake the basket or stir the wings for more even cooking.
5. Transfer the cooked wings to a plate in a single layer.
6. Sprinkle half of the Chinese five-spice powder on one side of the wings, then turn them over and sprinkle the other side with the remaining seasoning.

Charred Shishito Peppers

Servings: 4
Cooking Time: 5 Minutes

Ingredients:

- 20 shishito peppers (about 170g)
- 5ml vegetable oil
- Coarse sea salt
- 1 lemon

Directions:

1. Preheat the air fryer to 200°C (390°F).
2. Toss the shishito peppers with the vegetable oil and a sprinkle of coarse sea salt. You can do this in a bowl or directly in the air fryer basket.
3. Air-fry the shishito peppers at 200°C (390°F) for 5 minutes, shaking the basket once or twice during the cooking process to ensure even cooking.
4. Turn the charred peppers out into a bowl.

5. Squeeze some lemon juice over the top and season with coarse sea salt.
6. These should be served as finger foods - pick the pepper up by the stem and eat the whole pepper, seeds and all. Be cautious, as occasionally, you might encounter a spicy one!

Hot Avocado Fries

Servings: 2
Cooking Time: 20 Minutes
Ingredients:
- 1 egg
- 2 tablespoons milk
- Salt and pepper to taste
- 1 cup crushed chili corn chips
- 2 tablespoons Parmesan cheese
- 1 avocado, sliced into fries

Directions:
1. Preheat your air fryer to 190°C (375°F).
2. In a bowl, beat the egg and milk together. Season with salt and pepper to taste.
3. In another bowl, combine the crushed chili corn chips, Parmesan cheese, and additional salt and pepper if desired.
4. Dip the avocado fries into the egg mixture, ensuring they are well-coated.
5. Dredge the egg-coated avocado fries into the crushed chips and Parmesan cheese mixture, pressing the coating onto the fries to adhere.
6. Place the coated avocado fries in the greased air fryer basket in a single layer, making sure they are not touching.
7. Air fry the avocado fries for 5 minutes or until they are golden brown and crispy. You may need to do this in batches if your air fryer basket is small.
8. Serve the hot avocado fries immediately as a delicious snack or appetizer.

Hot Shrimp

Servings: 4
Cooking Time: 15 Minutes
Ingredients:
- 450g shrimp, cleaned and deveined
- 4 tbsp olive oil
- ½ lime, juiced
- 3 garlic cloves, minced
- ½ tsp salt
- ¼ tsp chili powder
- Instructions:
- Preheat your air fryer to 190°C (380°F).
- In a bowl, combine the shrimp with 30ml (2 tbsp) of olive oil, the juice of half a lime, one-third of the minced garlic, salt, and red chili powder. Toss the shrimp until they are evenly coated.
- In a small ramekin, mix the remaining olive oil and the rest of the minced garlic.
- Place the seasoned shrimp into the center of a piece of aluminum foil. Fold the sides of the foil up and crimp the edges to create a sealed aluminum foil packet, leaving the top open.
- Put the foil packet containing the shrimp into the air fryer basket.
- Air fry the shrimp for approximately 10-12 minutes, or until they are pink and fully cooked, shaking the basket or turning the packet halfway through cooking for even heating.
- Remove the shrimp from the foil packet and serve immediately.

Breaded Mozzarella Sticks

Servings: 6
Cooking Time: 25 Minutes
Ingredients:
- 30 ml flour
- 1 egg
- 15 ml milk
- 120 ml bread crumbs
- 1/4 tsp salt
- 1/4 tsp Italian seasoning
- 10 mozzarella sticks
- 10 ml olive oil
- 120 ml warm marinara sauce

Directions:
1. Place the flour in a bowl. In another bowl, beat the egg and milk together. In a third bowl, combine the breadcrumbs, salt, and Italian seasoning.
2. Cut the mozzarella sticks into thirds.
3. Roll each piece of mozzarella in the flour, then dredge it in the egg mixture, and finally roll it in the breadcrumb mixture. Shake off the excess between each step. Place the breaded mozzarella sticks in the freezer for 10 minutes to firm up.
4. Preheat the air fryer to 200°C (400°F).
5. Place the mozzarella sticks in the air fryer basket and air fry for 5 minutes, shaking the basket twice during cooking to ensure even cooking. Brush the mozzarella sticks with olive oil during the cooking process.
6. Serve the mozzarella sticks immediately with warm marinara sauce for dipping.

Buffalo French Fries

Servings: 6
Cooking Time: 35 Minutes
Ingredients:
- 3 large russet potatoes
- 30 ml buffalo sauce
- 30 ml extra-virgin olive oil
- Salt and pepper to taste

Directions:
1. Preheat the air fryer to 193°C (380°F).
2. Peel and cut the potatoes lengthwise into French fries.
3. Place the cut potatoes in a bowl and coat them with olive oil, salt, and pepper.
4. Air fry the potato fries for 10 minutes.
5. Shake the air fryer basket to redistribute the fries, and then continue cooking for an additional 5 minutes.
6. Serve the Buffalo French Fries immediately, drizzled with buffalo sauce.

Cheese Straws

Servings: 8
Cooking Time: 7 Minutes
Ingredients:
- All-purpose flour, for dusting
- One quarter of a thawed sheet (that is, a quarter of the sheet cut into two even pieces; wrap and refreeze the remainder) from a 490g box of frozen puff pastry
- 1 Large egg
- 30ml Water
- 30g Finely grated Parmesan cheese
- Up to 1 teaspoon Ground black pepper

Directions:
1. Preheat the air fryer to 200°C (400°F).
2. Dust a clean, dry work surface with flour. Place one of the quarter pieces of puff pastry on top, dust the pastry lightly with flour, and roll it out with a rolling pin to form a 15cm square.
3. Whisk the large egg and water together in a small or medium bowl until well combined. Brush the pastry square generously with this egg mixture.
4. Sprinkle each pastry square with 30g of grated Parmesan cheese and up to 1/2 teaspoon of ground black pepper.
5. Cut each square into 4 even strips. Take each strip and twist it into a cheese straw. Place the twisted cheese straws on a baking sheet.
6. Arrange as many cheese straws as will fit in the air fryer basket, leaving space for air to circulate. Typically, you can fit 4 straws in a small machine, 5 in a medium model, or 6 in a large one. Keep any remaining straws on a baking sheet in the fridge while each batch cooks.
7. Air-fry the cheese straws undisturbed for 7 minutes, or until they are puffed and crisp.
8. Use tongs to transfer the cheese straws to a wire rack, and then make subsequent batches in the same way (keeping the baking sheet with the remaining straws in the fridge as each batch cooks).
9. Serve the Cheese Straws warm.

Home-style Reuben Spread

Servings: 6
Cooking Time: 20 Minutes
Ingredients:
- 227 grams (8 oz) cream cheese, softened
- 225 grams (1 cup) chopped deli corned beef
- 60 ml (¼ cup) mayonnaise
- 60 ml (¼ cup) sour cream
- 235 ml (1 cup) drained sauerkraut
- 235 ml (1 cup) grated Gruyère cheese
- 5 ml (1 tsp) caraway seeds
- 30 ml (2 tbsp) parsley, chopped

Directions:
1. Preheat the air fryer to 200°C (400°F).
2. In a bowl, add the cream cheese, mayo, and sour cream, and stir until combined.
3. Add corned beef, sauerkraut, 120 ml (½ cup) of Gruyere cheese, parsley, and caraway seeds. Mix until well combined.
4. Spoon the mixture into a baking dish and top with the remaining 115 ml (½ cup) of Gruyere cheese.
5. Place the dish in the frying basket and Bake for 10 minutes.
6. Serve your Home-Style Reuben Spread.

Cinnamon Honeyed Pretzel Bites

Servings: 6
Cooking Time: 40 Minutes
Ingredients:
- 1 ½ tsp quick-rise yeast
- 2 tsp light brown sugar
- 1 tsp vanilla extract
- ½ tsp lemon zest
- 270g flour
- ½ tsp salt
- 7.5g honey
- 10g cinnamon powder

Directions:
1. Preheat the air fryer to 193°C (380°F).

2. Stir 175ml warm water and yeast in a medium bowl and let it sit for 5 minutes.
3. Combine the yeast water with 250g of flour, light brown sugar, vanilla extract, lemon zest, cinnamon, salt, and honey. Stir until a sticky dough forms.
4. Sprinkle the remaining flour (20g) on a flat work surface, then place the dough on the surface.
5. Knead the dough for 2-3 minutes or until it comes together in a smooth ball.
6. Divide the dough into 4 pieces. Roll each section into a log.
7. Cut each log into 5 pieces to make pretzel bites.
8. Arrange the dough pieces on the greased air fryer basket.
9. Bake for 3 minutes, then use tongs to flip the pretzel bites.
10. Cook for another 3-4 minutes or until the pretzel bites have browned.
11. Serve your Cinnamon Honeyed Pretzel Bites warm and enjoy.

Asian Rice Logs

Servings: 8
Cooking Time: 5 Minutes
Ingredients:
- 300 grams cooked jasmine or sushi rice
- 1/4 teaspoon salt
- 2 teaspoons five-spice powder
- 2 teaspoons diced shallots
- 15 ml tamari sauce
- 1 egg, beaten
- 5 ml sesame oil
- 10 ml water
- 80 grams plain breadcrumbs
- 90 grams panko breadcrumbs
- 2 tablespoons sesame seeds
- Orange Marmalade Dipping Sauce:
- 120 ml all-natural orange marmalade
- 15 ml soy sauce

Directions:
1. Cook the rice according to package instructions. While the rice is cooking, prepare the dipping sauce by combining the orange marmalade and soy sauce. Set the sauce aside.
2. In a mixing bowl, stir together the cooked rice, salt, five-spice powder, diced shallots, and tamari sauce.
3. Divide the rice mixture into 8 equal pieces. With slightly damp hands, shape each piece into a log shape. Chill the rice logs in the freezer for 10 to 15 minutes.
4. In a shallow bowl, mix the beaten egg, sesame oil, and water.
5. Place the plain breadcrumbs on a sheet of wax paper.
6. Mix the panko breadcrumbs with the sesame seeds and place them on another sheet of wax paper.
7. Roll each rice log in the plain breadcrumbs, then dip it in the egg wash, and finally coat it with the panko and sesame seed mixture.
8. Cook the rice logs in the air fryer at 200°C (390°F) for approximately 5 minutes or until they are golden brown.
9. Allow the cooked rice logs to cool slightly before serving them with the Orange Marmalade Dipping Sauce.

Herby Breaded Artichoke Hearts

Servings: 6
Cooking Time: 25 Minutes
Ingredients:
- 12 canned artichoke hearts
- 2 eggs
- 60g all-purpose flour
- 40g panko bread crumbs
- 1/2 tsp dried thyme
- 1/2 tsp dried parsley

Directions:
1. Preheat the air fryer to 193°C (380°F).
2. Set out three small bowls. In the first, add the flour. In the second, beat the eggs. In the third, mix the breadcrumbs, dried thyme, and dried parsley.
3. Dip each artichoke heart in the flour, then dredge it in the beaten eggs, and finally coat it with the breadcrumb mixture. Ensure they are coated evenly.
4. Place the breaded artichokes in the greased frying basket of the air fryer.
5. Air Fry for 8 minutes, flipping them once halfway through, until they are just browned and crisp.
6. Allow them to cool slightly before serving.

Hot Cheese Bites

Servings: 6
Cooking Time: 30 Minutes + Cooling Time
Ingredients:
- 1/3 cup grated Velveeta cheese
- 1/3 cup shredded American cheese
- 4 oz cream cheese
- 2 jalapeños, finely chopped
- ½ cup bread crumbs
- 2 egg whites
- ½ cup all-purpose flour

Directions:
1. Preheat your air fryer to 204°C (400°F).

2. In a mixing bowl, combine the cream cheese, Velveeta cheese, shredded American cheese, and finely chopped jalapeños. Mix until well blended.
3. Form the cheese mixture into 1-inch balls and place them on a sheet pan. Freeze the cheese balls for 15 minutes to firm them up.
4. While the cheese balls are in the freezer, prepare three separate bowls: one with all-purpose flour, one with egg whites, and one with bread crumbs.
5. Remove the cheese balls from the freezer and roll each one in the flour, then dip them into the egg whites, and finally coat them with the bread crumbs. Make sure they are evenly coated.
6. Grease the air fryer basket to prevent sticking, and place the coated cheese bites in the basket in a single layer.
7. Air fry the cheese bites at 204°C (400°F) for 8 minutes.
8. After 8 minutes, flip the cheese bites to ensure even cooking, and air fry for an additional 4 minutes or until they are crispy and golden brown.
9. Remove the hot cheese bites from the air fryer and allow them to cool slightly before serving.
10. Serve the Hot Cheese Bites as a delightful and cheesy appetizer.

Balsamic Grape Dip

Servings: 6
Cooking Time: 25 Minutes
Ingredients:
- 360 grams seedless red grapes
- 15 ml balsamic vinegar
- 15 ml honey
- 240 ml Greek yogurt
- 30 ml milk
- 30 ml minced fresh basil

Directions:
1. Preheat the air fryer to 190°C (380°F).
2. Add the seedless red grapes and balsamic vinegar to the air fryer basket. Pour the honey over the grapes and toss them to coat.
3. Roast the grapes in the air fryer for 8-12 minutes, until they shrivel, then remove them from the air fryer.
4. In a separate bowl, mix the milk and Greek yogurt together.
5. Gently stir the roasted grapes and minced fresh basil into the yogurt mixture.
6. Serve the Balsamic Grape Dip and enjoy!

Classic Potato Chips

Servings: 4
Cooking Time: 8 Minutes
Ingredients:
- 2 medium russet potatoes, washed
- 473 ml filtered water
- 15 ml avocado oil
- 2.5 ml salt

Directions:
1. Using a mandolin, slice the potatoes into 3 mm-thick pieces.
2. Pour the water into a large bowl. Place the potatoes in the bowl and soak for at least 30 minutes.
3. Preheat the air fryer to 175°C (350°F).
4. Drain the water and pat the potatoes dry with a paper towel or kitchen cloth. Toss with avocado oil and salt.
5. Liberally spray the air fryer basket with olive oil mist.
6. Set the potatoes inside the air fryer basket, separating them so they're not on top of each other.
7. Cook for 5 minutes, shake the basket, and cook for another 5 minutes, or until browned.
8. Remove and let cool a few minutes prior to serving. Repeat until all the chips are cooked.

Honey Tater Tots With Bacon

Servings: 4
Cooking Time: 25 Minutes
Ingredients:
- 24 frozen tater tots
- 6 bacon slices
- 15 ml (1 tbsp) honey
- 240 ml (1 cup) grated cheddar cheese

Directions:
1. Preheat the air fryer to 204°C (400°F).
2. Air Fry the frozen tater tots for 10 minutes, shaking the basket once halfway through cooking.
3. While the tater tots are cooking, cut the bacon into pieces.
4. When the tater tots are done, remove them from the air fryer and transfer them to a baking pan.
5. Top the tater tots with the bacon pieces and drizzle them with honey.
6. Air Fry for an additional 5 minutes to crisp up the bacon.
7. After that, top the tater tots with grated cheddar cheese and cook for an additional 2 minutes or until the cheese is melted.
8. Serve your Honey Tater Tots with Bacon.

Vegetarian & Vegan Recipes

Ratatouille

Servings: 4
Cooking Time:xx
Ingredients:
- ½ small aubergine, cubed
- 1 courgette, cubed
- 1 tomato, cubed
- 1 pepper, cut into cubes
- ½ onion, diced
- 1 fresh cayenne pepper, sliced
- 1 tsp vinegar
- 5 sprigs basil, chopped
- 2 sprigs oregano, chopped
- 1 clove garlic, crushed
- Salt and pepper
- 1 tbsp olive oil
- 1 tbsp white wine

Directions:
1. Preheat air fryer to 200ºC
2. Place all ingredients in a bowl and mix
3. Pour into a baking dish
4. Add dish to the air fryer and cook for 8 minutes, stir then cook for another 10 minutes

Baked Aubergine Slices With Yogurt Dressing

Servings: 2
Cooking Time:xx
Ingredients:
- 1 aubergine/eggplant, sliced 1.5 cm/⅝ in. thick
- 3 tablespoons olive oil
- ½ teaspoon salt
- YOGURT DRESSING
- 1 small garlic clove
- 1 tablespoon tahini or nut butter
- 100 g/½ cup Greek yogurt
- 2 teaspoons freshly squeezed lemon juice
- 1 tablespoon runny honey
- a pinch of salt
- a pinch of ground cumin
- a pinch of sumac
- TO SERVE
- 30 g/1 oz. rocket/arugula
- 2 tablespoons freshly chopped mint
- 3 tablespoons pomegranate seeds

Directions:
1. Preheat the air-fryer to 180ºC/350ºF.
2. Drizzle the olive oil over each side of the aubergine/eggplant slices. Sprinkle with salt. Add the aubergines to the preheated air-fryer and air-fry for 10 minutes, turning halfway through cooking.
3. Meanwhile, make the dressing by combining all the ingredients in a mini food processor (alterantively, finely chop the garlic, add to a jar with the other ingredients and shake vigorously).
4. Serve the cooked aubergine slices on a bed of rocket/arugula, drizzled with the dressing and with the mint and pomegranate seeds scattered over the top.

Veggie Bakes

Servings: 2
Cooking Time:xx
Ingredients:
- Any type of leftover vegetable bake you have
- 30g flour

Directions:
1. Preheat the air fryer to 180ºC
2. Mix the flour with the leftover vegetable bake
3. Shape into balls and place in the air fryer
4. Cook for 10 minutes

Aubergine Dip

Servings: 4
Cooking Time:xx
Ingredients:
- 1 aubergine
- 2 tsp oil
- 3 tbsp tahini
- 1 tbsp lemon juice
- 1 clove garlic minced
- ⅛ tsp cumin
- ¼ tsp smoked salt
- ⅛ tsp salt
- Drizzle olive oil

Directions:
1. Cut the aubergine in half length wise and coat in oil, Place in the air fryer and cook at 200ºC for 20 minutes
2. Remove from the air fryer and allow to cool
3. Scoop out the aubergine from the peel and put in a food processor

4. Add all the remaining ingredients, blend to combine but not to a puree
5. Serve with a drizzle of olive oil

Mushroom Pasta

Servings: 4
Cooking Time:xx
Ingredients:
- 250g sliced mushrooms
- 1 chopped onion
- 2 tsp minced garlic
- 1 tsp salt
- ½ tsp red pepper flakes
- 75g cup cream
- 70g mascarpone
- 1 tsp dried thyme
- 1 tsp ground black pepper
- ½ cup grated parmesan

Directions:
1. Place all the ingredients in a bowl and mix well
2. Heat the air fryer to 175°C
3. Grease a 7x3 inch pan and pour in the mixture
4. Place in the air fryer and cook for 15 minutes stirring halfway through
5. Pour over cooked pasta and sprinkle with parmesan

Bagel Pizza

Servings: 1
Cooking Time:xx
Ingredients:
- 1 bagel
- 2 tbsp marinara sauce
- 6 slices vegan pepperoni
- 2 tbsp mozzarella
- Pinch of basil

Directions:
1. Heat the air fryer to 180°C
2. Cut the bagel in half and toast for 2 minutes in the air fryer
3. Remove from the air fryer and top with marinara sauce, pepperoni and mozzarella
4. Return to the air fryer and cook for 4-5 minutes
5. Sprinkle with basil to serve

Lentil Balls With Zingy Rice

Servings: 4
Cooking Time:xx
Ingredients:
- 2 cans lentils
- 200g walnut halves
- 3 tbsp dried mushrooms
- 3 tbsp parsley
- 1 ½ tbsp tomato paste
- ¾ tsp salt
- ½ tsp pepper
- 100g bread crumbs
- 400ml water
- 200g rice
- 2 tbsp lemon juice
- 2 tsp lemon zest
- Salt to taste

Directions:
1. Preheat air fryer to 190°C
2. Place the lentils, walnuts, mushrooms, parsley, tomato paste, salt, pepper in a food processor and blend
3. Fold in the bread crumbs
4. Form the mix into balls and place in the air fryer
5. Cook for 10 minutes turn then cook for a further 5 minutes
6. Add the rice to a pan with water, bring to the boil and simmer for 20 minutes
7. Stir in the lemon juice, lemon zest and salt. Serve

Air-fried Artichoke Hearts

Servings: 7
Cooking Time:xx
Ingredients:
- 14 artichoke hearts
- 200g flour
- ¼ tsp baking powder
- Salt
- 6 tbsp water
- 6 tbsp breadcrumbs
- ¼ tsp basil
- ¼ tsp oregano
- ¼ tsp garlic powder
- ¼ tsp paprika

Directions:
1. Mix the baking powder, salt, flour and water in a bowl
2. In another bowl combine the breadcrumbs and seasonings
3. Dip the artichoke in the batter then coat in breadcrumbs
4. Place in the air fryer and cook at 180°C for 8 minutes

Camembert & Soldiers

Servings: 2
Cooking Time:xx
Ingredients:
- 1 piece of Camembert
- 2 slices sandwich bread
- 1 tbsp mustard

Directions:
1. Preheat the air fryer to 180ºC
2. Place the camembert in a sturdy container, cook in the air fryer for 15 minutes
3. Toast the bread and cut into soldiers
4. Serve with the mustard by the side

Sticky Tofu With Cauliflower Rice

Servings:4
Cooking Time:20 Minutes
Ingredients:
- For the tofu:
- 1 x 180 g / 6 oz block firm tofu
- 2 tbsp soy sauce
- 1 onion, sliced
- 1 large carrot, peeled and thinly sliced
- For the cauliflower:
- 200 g / 7 oz cauliflower florets
- 2 tbsp soy sauce
- 1 tbsp sesame oil
- 2 cloves garlic, minced
- 100 g / 3.5 oz broccoli, chopped into small florets

Directions:
1. Preheat the air fryer to 190 °C / 370 °F and line the air fryer with parchment paper or grease it with olive oil.
2. Crumble the tofu into a bowl and mix in the soy sauce, and the sliced onion and carrot.
3. Cook the tofu and vegetables in the air fryer for 10 minutes.
4. Meanwhile, place the cauliflower florets into a blender and pulse until it forms a rice-like consistency.
5. Place the cauliflower rice in a bowl and mix in the soy sauce, sesame oil, minced garlic cloves, and broccoli florets until well combined. Transfer to the air fryer and cook for 10 minutes until hot and crispy.

Chickpea And Sweetcorn Falafel

Servings:4
Cooking Time:15 Minutes
Ingredients:
- ½ onion, sliced
- 2 cloves garlic, peeled and sliced
- 2 tbsp fresh parsley, chopped
- 2 tbsp fresh coriander, chopped
- 2 x 400 g / 14 oz chickpeas, drained and rinsed
- 1 tsp salt
- 1 tsp black pepper
- 1 tsp baking powder
- 1 tsp dried mixed herbs
- 1 tsp cumin
- 1 tsp chili powder
- 50 g / 1.8 oz sweetcorn, fresh or frozen

Directions:
1. Preheat the air fryer to 180 °C / 350 °F and line the bottom of the basket with parchment paper.
2. In a food processor, place the onion, garlic cloves, fresh parsley, and fresh coriander. Pulse the ingredients in 30-second intervals until they form a smooth mixture. Scrape the mixture from the sides of the food processor in between each interval if necessary.
3. Mix in the chickpeas, salt, black pepper, baking powder, dried mixed herbs, cumin, and chili powder. Pulse the mixture until fully combined and smooth. Add more water if the mixture is looking a bit dry. The mixture should be dry but not crumbly.
4. Use a spoon to scoop out 2 tbsp of the chickpea mixture at a time and roll into small, even falafels.
5. Transfer the falafels into the prepared air fryer basket and cook for 12-15 minutes.
6. Serve the falafels either hot or cold as a side dish to your main meal or as part of a large salad.

Gnocchi Caprese

Servings: 2
Cooking Time:xx
Ingredients:
- 1 packet of gnocchi
- 150g cherry tomatoes, cut into halves
- 2 tbsp olive oil
- 2 tbsp balsamic vinegar
- 3 pressed cloves of garlic
- 200g basil, chopped
- 200g mini mozzarella balls
- 150g grated Parmesan
- Salt and pepper for seasoning

Directions:
1. Preheat the air fryer to 220ºC
2. Take a large bowl and add the cherry tomatoes, gnocchi, oil, balsamic vinegar, garlic and seasoning, making sure that everything is well coated

3. Transfer to the air fryer basket
4. Cook for 10 minutes, shaking the basket every few minutes
5. Once cooked, transfer everything to a large mixing bowl and add the Parmesan cheese, coating well
6. Then, add the mozzarella and basil and toss once more

Broccoli Cheese

Servings: 2
Cooking Time:xx
Ingredients:
- 250g broccoli
- Cooking spray
- 10 tbsp evaporated milk
- 300g Mexican cheese
- 4 tsp Amarillo paste
- 6 saltine crackers

Directions:
1. Heat the air fryer to 190°C
2. Place the broccoli in the air fryer spray with cooking oil and cook for about 6 minutes
3. Place the remaining ingredients in a blender and process until smooth
4. Place in a bowl and microwave for 30 seconds
5. Pour over the broccoli and serve

Mini Quiche

Servings: 2
Cooking Time:xx
Ingredients:
- 100g raw cashews
- 3 tbsp milk
- ½ tsp hot sauce
- 1 tsp white miso paste
- 1 tsp mustard
- 300g tofu
- 100g bacon pieces
- 1 chopped red pepper
- 1 chopped onion
- 6 tbsp yeast
- ½ tsp onion powder
- ½ tsp paprika
- ½ tsp cumin
- ½ tsp chilli powder
- ½ tsp black pepper
- ⅛ tsp turmeric
- ½ tsp canola oil
- 50g curly kale

Directions:
1. Heat the oil in a pan, add the bacon pepper, onion and curly kale and cook for about 3 minutes
2. Place all the other ingredients into a blender and blend until smooth
3. Add to a bowl with the bacon, pepper, onion and curly kale and mix well
4. Fill silicone muffin cups with the mix
5. Place in the air fryer and cook at 165°C for 15 minutes

Rainbow Vegetables

Servings: 4
Cooking Time:xx
Ingredients:
- 1 red pepper, cut into slices
- 1 squash sliced
- 1 courgette sliced
- 1 tbsp olive oil
- 150g sliced mushrooms
- 1 onion sliced
- Salt and pepper to taste

Directions:
1. Preheat air fryer to 180°C
2. Place all ingredients in a bowl and mix well
3. Place in the air fryer and cook for about 20 minutes turning halfway

Butternut Squash Falafel

Servings: 2
Cooking Time:xx
Ingredients:
- 500 g/1 lb. 2 oz. frozen butternut squash cubes
- 1 tablespoon olive oil, plus extra for cooking
- 100 g/¾ cup canned or cooked chickpeas (drained weight)
- 20 g/¼ cup gram/chickpea flour
- 1 teaspoon ground cumin
- ½ teaspoon ground coriander
- ½ teaspoon salt

Directions:
1. Preheat the air-fryer to 180°C/350°F.
2. Toss the frozen butternut squash in the olive oil. Add to the preheated air-fryer and air-fry for 12–14 minutes, until soft but not caramelized. Remove from the air-fryer and mash the squash by hand or using a food processor, then combine with the chickpeas, flour, spices and salt. Leave the mixture to cool, then divide into 6 equal portions and mould into patties.
3. Preheat the air-fryer to 180°C/350°F.

4. Spray the patties with a little olive oil, then add to the preheated air-fryer and air-fry for 10 minutes, turning once (carefully) during cooking. Enjoy hot or cold.

Paneer Tikka

Servings: 2
Cooking Time:xx
Ingredients:
- 200ml yogurt
- 1 tsp ginger garlic paste
- 1 tsp red chilli powder
- 1 tsp garam masala
- 1 tsp turmeric powder
- 1 tbsp dried fenugreek leaves
- The juice of 1 lemon
- 2 tbsp chopped coriander
- 1 tbsp olive oil
- 250g paneer cheese, cut into cubes
- 1 green pepper, chopped
- 1 red pepper, chopped
- 1 yellow pepper, chopped
- 1 chopped onion

Directions:
1. Take a mixing bowl and add the yogurt, garlic paste, red chilli powder, garam masala, turmeric powder, lemon juice, fenugreek and chopped coriander, combining well
2. Place the marinade to one side
3. Add the cubed cheese to the marinade and toss to coat well
4. Leave to marinade for 2 hours
5. Take 8 skewers and alternate the cheese with the peppers and onions
6. Drizzle a little oil over the top
7. Arrange in the air fryer and cook at 220ºC for 3 minutes
8. Turn and cook for another 3 minutes

Sweet Potato Taquitos

Servings: 10
Cooking Time:xx
Ingredients:
- 1 sweet potato cut into ½ inch pieces
- 1 ½ tsp oil
- 1 chopped onion
- 1 tsp minced garlic
- 400g black beans
- 3 tbsp water
- 10 corn tortillas
- 1 chipotle pepper, chopped
- ½ tsp cumin
- ½ tsp paprika
- ½ chilli powder
- ⅛ tsp salt
- ½ tsp maple syrup

Directions:
1. Place the sweet potato in the air fryer spray with oil and cook for 12 minutes at 200ºC
2. Heat oil in a pan, add the onion and garlic and cook for a few minutes until soft
3. Add remaining ingredients to the pan, add 2 tbsp of water and combine
4. Add the sweet potato and 1 tbsp of water and mix
5. Warm the tortilla in the microwave for about 1 minute
6. Place a row of filling across the centre of each tortilla. Fold up the bottom of the tortilla, tuck under the filling, fold in the edges then continue to roll the tortilla
7. Place in the air fryer and cook for about 12 minutes

Spring Ratatouille

Servings:2
Cooking Time:15 Minutes
Ingredients:
- 1 tbsp olive oil
- 4 Roma tomatoes, sliced
- 2 cloves garlic, minced
- 1 courgette, cut into chunks
- 1 red pepper and 1 yellow pepper, cut into chunks
- 2 tbsp mixed herbs
- 1 tbsp vinegar

Directions:
1. Preheat the air fryer to 190 °C / 370 °F and line the air fryer with parchment paper or grease it with olive oil.
2. Place all of the ingredients into a large mixing bowl and mix until fully combined.
3. Transfer the vegetables into the lined air fryer basket, close the lid, and cook for 15 minutes until the vegetables have softened.

Spinach And Egg Air Fryer Breakfast Muffins

Servings:4
Cooking Time:10 Minutes
Ingredients:
- 8 eggs
- 100 g / 3.5 oz fresh spinach
- 50 g / 1.8 oz cheddar cheese, grated
- ½ onion, finely sliced

- 1 tsp black pepper

Directions:
1. Preheat your air fryer to 200 °C / 400 °F and line an 8-pan muffin tray with parchment paper or grease with olive oil.
2. Gently press the spinach leaves into the bottom of each prepared muffin cup.
3. Sprinkle the finely sliced onion on top of the spinach.
4. Crack 2 eggs into each cup on top of the spinach and add some of the grated cheddar cheese on top of the eggs. Top with a light sprinkle of black pepper.
5. Carefully place the muffins into the air fryer basket and shut the lid. Bake for 10 minutes until the eggs are set and the muffins are hot throughout.
6. Serve the muffins while still hot for breakfast.

Vegetarian "chicken" Tenders

Servings: 4
Cooking Time: xx

Ingredients:
- 250g flour
- 3 eggs
- 100g panko bread crumbs
- 1 tsp garlic powder
- 2 packs of vegetarian chicken breasts
- ¾ tsp paprika
- ½ tsp cayenne
- ½ tsp pepper
- ½ tsp chilli powder
- ½ tsp salt

Directions:
1. Pour flour onto a plate, beat eggs into a bowl. Combine all remaining dry ingredients in a bowl
2. Cut the chicken into strips
3. Dip the chicken in flour, then egg and then into the breadcrumb mix
4. Heat the air fryer to 260ºC
5. Cook for 6 minutes turn and then cook for another 6 minutes until golden brown

Flat Mushroom Pizzas

Servings: 1
Cooking Time: xx

Ingredients:
- 2 portobello mushrooms, cleaned and stalk removed
- 6 mozzarella balls
- 1 teaspoon olive oil
- PIZZA SAUCE
- 100 g/3½ oz. passata/strained tomatoes
- 1 teaspoon dried oregano
- ¼ teaspoon garlic salt

Directions:
1. Preheat the air-fryer to 180ºC/350ºF.
2. Mix the ingredients for the pizza sauce together in a small bowl. Fill each upturned portobello mushroom with sauce, then top each with three mozzarella balls and drizzle the olive oil over.
3. Add the mushrooms to the preheated air-fryer and air-fry for 8 minutes. Serve immediately.

Orange Zingy Cauliflower

Servings: 2
Cooking Time: xx

Ingredients:
- 200ml water
- 200g flour
- Half the head of a cauliflower, cut into 1.5" florets
- 2 tsp olive oil
- 2 minced garlic cloves
- 1 tsp minced ginger
- 150ml orange juice
- 3 tbsp white vinegar
- 1/2 tsp red pepper flakes
- 1 tsp sesame oil 100g brown sugar
- 3 tbsp soy sauce
- 1 tbsp cornstarch
- 2 tbsp water
- 1 tsp salt

Directions:
1. Take a medium mixing bowl and add the water, salt and flour together
2. Dip each floret of cauliflower into the mixture and place in the air fryer basket
3. Cook at 220ºC for 15 minutes
4. Meanwhile make the orange sauce by combining all ingredients in a saucepan and allowing to simmer for 3 minutes, until the sauce has thickened
5. Drizzle the sauce over the cauliflower to serve

Arancini

Servings: 12
Cooking Time: xx

Ingredients:
- 1 batch of risotto
- 100g panko breadcrumbs
- 1 tsp onion powder
- Salt and pepper

- 300ml warm marinara sauce

Directions:
1. Take ¼ cup risotto and form a rice ball
2. Mix the panko crumbs, onion powder, salt and pepper
3. Coat the risotto ball in the crumb mix
4. Place in the air fryer, spray with oil and cook at 200ºC for 10 minutes
5. Serve with marinara sauce

Spicy Spanish Potatoes

Servings: 2
Cooking Time:xx

Ingredients:
- 4 large potatoes
- 1 tbsp olive oil
- 2 tsp paprika
- 2 tsp dried garlic
- 1 tsp barbacoa seasoning
- Salt and pepper

Directions:
1. Chop the potatoes into wedges
2. Place them in a bowl with olive oil and seasoning, mix well
3. Add to the air fryer and cook at 160ºC for 20 minutes
4. Shake, increase heat to 200ºC and cook for another 3 minutes

Courgette Burgers

Servings: 4
Cooking Time:xx

Ingredients:
- 1 courgette
- 1 small can of chickpeas, drained
- 3 spring onions
- Pinch of dried garlic
- Salt and pepper
- 3 tbsp coriander
- 1 tsp chilli powder
- 1 tsp mixed spice
- 1 tsp cumin

Directions:
1. Grate the courgette and drain the excess water
2. Thinly slice the spring onions and add to the bowl with the chickpeas, courgette and seasoning
3. Bind the ingredients and form into patties
4. Place in the air fryer and cook for 12 minutes at 200ºC

Spinach And Feta Croissants

Servings:4
Cooking Time:10 Minutes

Ingredients:
- 4 pre-made croissants
- 100 g / 7 oz feta cheese, crumbled
- 1 tsp dried chives
- 1 tsp garlic powder
- 50 g / 3.5 oz fresh spinach, chopped

Directions:
1. Preheat the air fryer to 180 °C / 350 °F. Remove the mesh basket from the air fryer machine and line with parchment paper.
2. Cut the croissants in half and lay each half out on the lined mesh basket.
3. In a bowl, combine the crumbled feta cheese, dried chives, garlic powder, and chopped spinach until they form a consistent mixture.
4. Spoon some of the mixture one half of the four croissants and cover with the second half of the croissants to seal in the filling.
5. Carefully slide the croissants in the mesh basket into the air fryer machine, close the lid, and cook for 10 minutes until the pastry is crispy and the feta cheese has melted.

Roast Cauliflower & Broccoli

Servings: 6
Cooking Time:xx

Ingredients:
- 300g broccoli
- 300g cauliflower
- 2 tbsp oil
- ½ tsp garlic powder
- ¼ tsp salt
- ¼ tsp paprika
- ⅛ tsp pepper

Directions:
1. Preheat air fryer to 200ºC
2. Place broccoli and cauliflower in a bowl and microwave for 3 minutes
3. Add remaining ingredients and mix well
4. Add to the air fryer and cook for about 12 mins

Lentil Burgers

Servings: 4
Cooking Time:xx

Ingredients:
- 100g black buluga lentils
- 1 carrot, grated
- 1 diced onion
- 100g white cabbage

- 300g oats
- 1 tbsp garlic puree
- 1 tsp cumin
- Salt and pepper

Directions:
1. Blend the oats until they resemble flour
2. Put the lentils in a pan with water and cook for 45 minutes
3. Steam your vegetables for 5 minutes
4. Add all the ingredients into a bowl and mix well to combine
5. Form into burgers place in the air fryer and cook at 180°C for 30 minutes

Whole Wheat Pizza

Servings: 2
Cooking Time:xx

Ingredients:
- 100g marinara sauce
- 2 whole wheat pitta
- 200g baby spinach leaves
- 1 small plum tomato, sliced
- 1 clove garlic, sliced
- 400g grated cheese
- 50g shaved parmesan

Directions:
1. Preheat air fryer to 160°C
2. Spread each of the pitta with marinara sauce
3. Sprinkle with cheese, top with spinach, plum tomato and garlic. Finish with parmesan shavings
4. Place in the air fryer and cook for about 4 mins cheese has melted

Vegan Fried Ravioli

Servings: 4
Cooking Time:xx

Ingredients:
- 100g panko breadcrumbs
- 2 tsp yeast
- 1 tsp basil
- 1 tsp oregano
- 1 tsp garlic powder
- Pinch salt and pepper
- 50ml liquid from can of chickpeas
- 150g vegan ravioli
- Cooking spray
- 50g marinara for dipping

Directions:
1. Combine the breadcrumbs, yeast, basil, oregano, garlic powder and salt and pepper
2. Put the liquid from the chickpeas in a bowl
3. Dip the ravioli in the liquid then dip into the breadcrumb mix
4. Heat the air fryer to 190°C
5. Place the ravioli in the air fryer and cook for about 6 minutes until crispy

Beef, pork & Lamb Recipes

Crispy Pierogi With Kielbasa And Onions

Servings: 3
Cooking Time: 20 Minutes
Ingredients:
- 6 Frozen potato and cheese pierogi, thawed (about 12 pierogi to 1 pound)
- 225g Smoked kielbasa, sliced into 1.25cm-thick rounds
- 180ml Very roughly chopped sweet onion, preferably Vidalia
- Vegetable oil spray

Directions:
1. Preheat your air fryer to 190°C (375°F).
2. Place the pierogi, kielbasa rounds, and chopped sweet onion in a large bowl.
3. Coat them with vegetable oil spray, toss well, spray again, and toss until everything is evenly coated.
4. When the machine is at temperature, transfer the contents of the bowl into the air fryer basket. Items may be leaning against each other and even on top of each other.
5. Air-fry, tossing and rearranging everything twice during the cooking process to ensure all covered surfaces get exposed, for 20 minutes, or until the sausages have begun to brown and the pierogi are crispy.
6. Pour the contents of the basket onto a serving platter. Wait for a minute or two to ensure nothing's searing hot before serving.

Exotic Pork Skewers

Servings: 4
Cooking Time: 30 Minutes
Ingredients:
- 80ml apricot jam
- 30ml lemon juice
- 10ml olive oil
- ½ tsp dried tarragon
- 450g pork tenderloin, cubed
- 4 pitted cherries, halved
- 4 pitted apricots, halved

Directions:
1. Preheat your air fryer to 190°C (380°F).
2. In a large bowl, combine the apricot jam, lemon juice, olive oil, and dried tarragon. Mix thoroughly to create a marinade.
3. Add the cubed pork tenderloin to the bowl with the marinade. Stir well to ensure the pork is evenly coated. Allow it to marinate for about 10 minutes.
4. Prepare metal skewers by poking them through the marinated pork, cherries, and apricot halves, alternating the ingredients to create skewers.
5. Use a cooking brush to apply the remaining marinade onto the skewers.
6. Place the skewers in the preheated air fryer basket.
7. Air fry the pork skewers at 190°C (380°F) for 4-6 minutes on each side, or until the pork is cooked through, and the fruit is soft and slightly caramelized.
8. Once cooked, remove the skewers from the air fryer.
9. Serve the Exotic Pork Skewers immediately, and enjoy the delicious combination of flavors!

Calzones South Of The Border

Servings: 8
Cooking Time: 8 Minutes
Ingredients:
- Filling:
- 115g ground pork sausage
- 2.5ml chile powder
- 1.25ml ground cumin
- 0.625ml garlic powder
- 0.625ml onion powder
- 0.625ml oregano
- 120ml ricotta cheese
- 28g sharp Cheddar cheese, shredded
- 56g Pepper Jack cheese, shredded
- 113g can chopped green chiles, drained
- Oil for misting or cooking spray
- Salsa, sour cream, or guacamole for serving
- Crust:
- 250g white wheat flour, plus more for kneading and rolling
- 7g package RapidRise yeast
- 5ml salt
- 2.5ml chile powder
- 2.5ml ground cumin
- 240ml warm water (46°C to 52°C)
- 10ml olive oil

Directions:
1. Crumble the sausage into the air fryer baking pan and stir in the filling seasonings: chile powder, cumin, garlic

powder, onion powder, and oregano. Cook at 200°C (390°F) for 2 minutes. Stir, breaking apart, and cook for an additional 3 to 4 minutes until well done. Remove and set aside on paper towels to drain.

2. To make the dough, combine flour, yeast, salt, chile powder, and cumin. Stir in warm water and oil until a soft dough forms. Turn it out onto a lightly floured board and knead for 3 or 4 minutes. Let the dough rest for 10 minutes.

3. Place the three cheeses in a medium bowl. Add the cooked sausage and chiles, then stir until well mixed.

4. Cut the dough into 8 pieces.

5. Working with 4 pieces of the dough at a time, press each into a circle about 12.7cm (5 inches) in diameter. Top each dough circle with 2 heaping tablespoons of filling. Fold it over into a half-moon shape and press the edges together firmly to prevent leakage. Spray both sides with oil or cooking spray.

6. Place 4 calzones in the air fryer basket and cook at 180°C (360°F) for 5 minutes. Mist with oil or spray and cook for an additional 3 minutes until the crust is done and nicely browned.

7. While the first batch is cooking, press out the remaining dough, fill, and shape into calzones.

8. Spray both sides with oil or cooking spray and cook for 5 minutes. If needed, mist with oil and continue cooking for an additional 3 minutes longer. This second batch will cook a little faster than the first because your air fryer is already hot.

9. Serve the Calzones South of the Border plain or with salsa, sour cream, or guacamole.

Baharat Lamb Kebab With Mint Sauce

Servings: 6
Cooking Time: 50 Minutes
Ingredients:
- 450 grams ground lamb
- 60 ml parsley, chopped
- 3 garlic cloves, minced
- 1 shallot, diced
- Salt and pepper to taste
- 5 grams ground cumin
- 1/4 teaspoon ground cinnamon
- 1/4 teaspoon baharat seasoning
- 1/4 teaspoon chili powder
- 1/4 teaspoon ground ginger
- 45 ml olive oil
- 240 ml Greek yogurt
- 120 ml mint, chopped

- 30 ml lemon juice
- 1/4 teaspoon hot paprika

Directions:
1. Preheat the air fryer to 180°C (360°F).
2. In a bowl, mix together the ground lamb, chopped parsley, 2 minced garlic cloves, diced shallot, 30 ml (2 tbsp) olive oil, salt, black pepper, ground cumin, ground cinnamon, baharat seasoning, chili powder, and ground ginger.
3. Divide the lamb mixture into 4 equal portions and roll each portion into a long oval shape.
4. Drizzle the remaining 15 ml (1 tbsp) of olive oil over the lamb ovals.
5. Place the lamb ovals in a single layer in the air fryer basket.
6. Air fry for 10 minutes, ensuring they cook evenly.
7. While the kofta is cooking, prepare the mint sauce by mixing together Greek yogurt, chopped mint, the remaining minced garlic clove, lemon juice, hot paprika, salt, and pepper in a bowl.
8. Serve the Baharat Lamb Kebab with the mint sauce.

Brie And Cranberry Burgers

Servings: 3
Cooking Time: 9 Minutes
Ingredients:
- 450 grams (1 pound) ground beef (80% lean)
- 15 ml (1 tablespoon) chopped fresh thyme
- 15 ml (1 tablespoon) Worcestershire sauce
- 2.5 ml (1/2 teaspoon) salt
- Freshly ground black pepper
- 113 grams (4-ounce) wheel of Brie cheese, sliced
- Handful of arugula
- 3 or 4 brioche hamburger buns (or potato hamburger buns), toasted
- 60 to 120 ml (1/4 to 1/2 cup) whole berry cranberry sauce

Directions:
1. Combine the ground beef, chopped fresh thyme, Worcestershire sauce, salt, and freshly ground black pepper in a large bowl. Mix well. Divide the meat into 3 (approximately 1/4-pound) portions and then form them into burger patties, being careful not to over-handle the meat.
2. Preheat the air fryer to 200°C (390°F) and pour a little water into the bottom of the air fryer drawer (to prevent grease from burning and smoking).
3. Transfer the burger patties to the air fryer basket. Air-fry the burgers at 200°C (390°F) for 5 minutes. Flip the burgers over and air-fry for another 2 minutes. Top each burger with

a couple of slices of Brie cheese and air-fry for another minute or two, just to soften the cheese.

4. Build the burgers by placing a few leaves of arugula on the bottom bun, adding the burger patty, and spooning cranberry sauce on top. Top with the other half of the hamburger bun and enjoy.

Cheesy Mushroom-stuffed Pork Loins

Servings: 3
Cooking Time: 30 Minutes
Ingredients:
- 180ml diced mushrooms
- 10ml olive oil
- 1 shallot, diced
- Salt and pepper to taste
- 3 center-cut pork loins
- 6 Gruyère cheese slices

Directions:
1. Warm the olive oil in a skillet over medium heat. Add the diced shallot and mushrooms and stir-fry for 3 minutes. Sprinkle with salt and pepper and cook for an additional 1 minute.
2. Preheat your air fryer to 180°C (350°F).
3. Cut a pocket into each pork loin and set them aside.
4. Stuff an even amount of the mushroom mixture into each chop pocket and top it with 2 Gruyère cheese slices in each pocket.
5. Place the stuffed pork loins in the lightly greased frying basket of the air fryer.
6. Air fry for 11 minutes or until the pork is cooked through and the cheese has melted.
7. Let the stuffed pork loins sit on a cutting board for 5 minutes before serving.

Easy Carnitas

Servings: 3
Cooking Time: 25 Minutes
Ingredients:
- 680g Boneless country-style pork ribs, cut into 5cm pieces
- 60ml Orange juice
- 2 tablespoons Brine from a jar of pickles, any type, even pickled jalapeño rings (gluten-free, if a concern)
- 2 teaspoons Minced garlic
- 2 teaspoons Minced fresh oregano leaves
- ¾ teaspoon Ground cumin
- ¾ teaspoon Table salt
- ¾ teaspoon Ground black pepper

Directions:
1. In a large bowl, mix the pieces of boneless country-style pork ribs with the orange juice, pickle brine, minced garlic, minced fresh oregano leaves, ground cumin, table salt, and ground black pepper. Ensure the pork pieces are well coated. Cover the bowl and refrigerate for at least 2 hours or up to 10 hours, stirring the mixture occasionally.
2. Preheat your air fryer to 200°C (400°F). Allow the rib pieces to sit in their bowl on the counter while the machine heats up.
3. Use kitchen tongs to transfer the marinated rib pieces to the air fryer basket, arranging them in a single layer. It's okay if some pieces touch.
4. Air-fry the pork pieces for 25 minutes, turning and rearranging them at the 10- and 20-minute marks to ensure that all surfaces are exposed to the air currents. Cook until the pieces are browned and sizzling.
5. Using clean kitchen tongs, transfer the cooked rib pieces to a wire rack. Allow them to cool for a couple of minutes before serving.

Carne Asada Recipes

Servings: 4
Cooking Time: 15 Minutes
Ingredients:
- 4 cloves garlic, minced
- 3 chipotle peppers in adobo, chopped
- 80ml chopped fresh parsley
- 80ml chopped fresh oregano
- 5ml ground cumin seed
- Juice of 2 limes
- 80ml olive oil
- 450g to 680g flank steak (depending on your appetite)
- Salt
- Tortillas and guacamole (optional – for serving)

Directions:
1. Make the marinade: Combine the minced garlic, chopped chipotle peppers, fresh parsley, fresh oregano, ground cumin, lime juice, and olive oil in a non-reactive bowl.
2. Coat the flank steak with the marinade and let it marinate for 30 minutes to 8 hours. Make sure not to leave the steak out of refrigeration for longer than 2 hours.
3. Preheat your air fryer to 200°C (390°F).
4. Remove the steak from the marinade and place it in the air fryer basket.
5. Season the steak with salt.
6. Air-fry the steak for 15 minutes, turning the steak over halfway through the cooking time and seasoning it again

with salt. This should cook the steak to medium. Adjust the time by adding or subtracting two minutes for medium-well or medium-rare, depending on your preference.

7. Remember to let the steak rest before slicing the meat against the grain.

8. Serve your Carne Asada with warm tortillas, guacamole, and a fresh salsa, like the Tomato-Corn Salsa below.

Ground Beef Calzones

Servings: 6
Cooking Time: 30 Minutes
Ingredients:
- 1 refrigerated pizza dough
- 225g shredded mozzarella
- 120g chopped onion
- 2 garlic cloves, minced
- 60g chopped mushrooms
- 450g ground beef
- 15ml pizza seasoning
- Salt and pepper to taste
- 355ml marinara sauce
- 5ml flour

Directions:

1. Heat 15ml of oil in a skillet over medium heat. Sauté the chopped onion, minced garlic, and chopped mushrooms for 2-3 minutes or until fragrant.

2. Add the ground beef, pizza seasoning, salt, and pepper. Use a large spoon to break up the beef. Cook for 3 minutes or until browned.

3. Stir in the marinara sauce and set the mixture aside.

4. On a floured work surface, roll out the pizza dough and cut it into 6 equal-sized rectangles.

5. On each rectangle, add 120ml of the beef mixture and top it with 15ml of shredded cheese.

6. Fold one side of the dough over the filling to the opposite side, creating a calzone. Press the edges using the back of a fork to seal them.

7. Preheat your air fryer to 200°C (400°F).

8. Place the first batch of calzones in the air fryer and spray them with cooking oil.

9. Bake for 10 minutes or until they are golden brown and crispy.

10. Let the calzones cool slightly before serving. Enjoy your delicious Ground Beef Calzones!

Better-than-chinese-take-out Sesame Beef

Servings: 4
Cooking Time: 14 Minutes
Ingredients:
- 565 grams (1 1/4 pounds) Beef flank steak
- 37.5 ml (2 1/2 tablespoons) Regular or low-sodium soy sauce or gluten-free tamari sauce
- 30 ml (2 tablespoons) Toasted sesame oil
- 7.5 ml (2 1/2 teaspoons) Cornstarch
- 480 grams (about 4 1/2 cups) Frozen mixed vegetables for stir-fry, thawed, seasoning packet discarded
- 45 ml (3 tablespoons) Unseasoned rice vinegar
- 45 ml (3 tablespoons) Thai sweet chili sauce
- 30 ml (2 tablespoons) Light brown sugar
- 30 ml (2 tablespoons) White sesame seeds
- 10 ml (2 teaspoons) Water
- Vegetable oil spray
- 22.5 ml (1 1/2 tablespoons) Minced peeled fresh ginger
- 15 ml (1 tablespoon) Minced garlic

Directions:

1. Place the flank steak on a cutting board and determine the direction of the meat's grain by running your clean fingers across it. Cut the flank steak into three pieces parallel to the meat's grain. Then cut each of these pieces into 25 cm (1/2-inch) wide strips against the grain.

2. Put the meat strips in a large bowl. For a small batch, add 10 ml (2 teaspoons) of the soy or tamari sauce, 10 ml (2 teaspoons) of the sesame oil, and 5 ml (1/2 teaspoon) of cornstarch; for a medium batch, add 15 ml (1 tablespoon) of the soy or tamari sauce, 15 ml (1 tablespoon) of the sesame oil, and 5 ml (1 teaspoon) of cornstarch; and for a large batch, add 22.5 ml (1 1/2 tablespoons) of the soy or tamari sauce, 22.5 ml (1 1/2 tablespoons) of the sesame oil, and 7.5 ml (1 1/2 teaspoons) of cornstarch. Toss well until the meat is thoroughly coated in the marinade. Set aside at room temperature.

3. Preheat the air fryer to 200°C (400°F).

4. When the machine reaches temperature, place the beef strips in the basket as closely as possible to form a single layer. The strips may overlap or cover each other. Air-fry for 10 minutes, tossing and rearranging the strips three times to ensure even browning and slight crispiness. Transfer the strips to a clean bowl.

5. Spread the thawed mixed vegetables in the basket and air-fry undisturbed for 4 minutes, just until they are heated through and somewhat softened. Transfer these to the bowl with the meat strips. Turn off the air fryer.

6. In a small bowl, whisk together the rice vinegar, sweet chili sauce, brown sugar, sesame seeds, the remaining soy sauce, and the remaining sesame oil until well combined. For a small batch, whisk the remaining 2.5 ml (1/2 teaspoon) of cornstarch with the water in a second small bowl to create a smooth slurry; for a medium batch, whisk the remaining 5 ml (1 teaspoon) of cornstarch with the water in a second small bowl to create a smooth slurry; and for a large batch, whisk the remaining 7.5 ml (1 1/2 teaspoons) of cornstarch with the water in a second small bowl to create a smooth slurry.

7. Generously coat the inside of a large wok with vegetable oil spray and heat the wok over high heat for a few minutes. Add the minced ginger and garlic, stir-frying for about 10 seconds until fragrant. Add the meat and vegetables, and stir-fry for 1 minute to heat through.

8. Pour in the rice vinegar mixture and continue stir-frying until the sauce begins to bubble, which should take less than 1 minute. Add the cornstarch slurry and stir-fry for just a few seconds until the sauce thickens.

9. Remove the wok from the heat and serve hot.

Authentic Sausage Kartoffel Salad

Servings: 4
Cooking Time: 50 Minutes
Ingredients:
- 225 grams cooked Polish sausage, sliced
- 2 cooked potatoes, cubed
- 240 ml chicken broth
- 2 tbsp olive oil
- 1 onion, chopped
- 2 garlic cloves, minced
- 60 ml apple cider vinegar
- 3 tbsp light brown sugar
- 2 tbsp cornstarch
- 60 ml sour cream
- 1 tsp yellow mustard
- 2 tbsp chopped chives

Directions:
1. Preheat the air fryer to 190°C (370°F).
2. In a baking pan, combine olive oil, chopped onion, minced garlic, and sliced sausage. Place the pan in the air fryer basket.
3. Air fry for 4-7 minutes or until the onions are crispy but tender, and the sausages are hot.
4. In a separate bowl, mix together the chicken broth, apple cider vinegar, light brown sugar, and cornstarch.
5. Pour this mixture into the pan with the sausage and onions. Stir well.
6. Continue air frying for an additional 5 minutes or until the mixture is hot and thickened.
7. Stir in the sour cream and yellow mustard until well combined.
8. Add the cubed cooked potatoes to the mixture and stir to coat.
9. Cook for another 2-3 minutes or until everything is hot and well combined.
10. Serve your Authentic Sausage Kartoffel Salad, topped with freshly chopped chives.

German-style Pork Patties

Servings: 6
Cooking Time: 35 Minutes
Ingredients:
- 450g ground pork
- 30g diced fresh pear
- 15g minced sage leaves
- 1 garlic clove, minced
- 30g chopped chives
- Salt and pepper to taste

Directions:
1. Preheat your air fryer to 190°C (375°F).
2. In a bowl, combine the ground pork, diced fresh pear, minced sage leaves, minced garlic, chopped chives, salt, and pepper. Gently mix the ingredients until thoroughly combined.
3. Shape the mixture into 8 patties, each about 1.3cm (½ inch) thick.
4. Arrange the patties in the greased air fryer basket in a single layer.
5. Air fry for 15-20 minutes, flipping the patties once halfway through the cooking time.
6. Remove the cooked patties from the air fryer and drain them on paper towels to remove excess oil.
7. Serve your German-Style Pork Patties and enjoy!

Crispy Pork Escalopes

Servings: 4
Cooking Time: 20 Minutes
Ingredients:
- 4 pork loin steaks
- Salt and pepper to taste
- 30g flour
- 2 tbsp bread crumbs

Directions:
1. Preheat the air fryer to 190°C (380°F).
2. Season the pork loin steaks with salt and pepper to taste.

3. In one shallow bowl, add the flour. In another shallow bowl, add the bread crumbs.
4. Dip each pork steak first in the flour, ensuring it's coated evenly, and then in the bread crumbs, pressing lightly to adhere the crumbs to the pork.
5. Place the breaded pork steaks in the preheated air fryer basket in a single layer. Spray them with a light coat of cooking oil.
6. Air fry for 12-14 minutes, flipping the steaks once during cooking, until they are crisp and cooked through.
7. Serve your crispy pork escalopes immediately.

Extra Crispy Country-style Pork Riblets

Servings: 3
Cooking Time: 30 Minutes
Ingredients:
- 80g Tapioca flour
- 37.5ml Chile powder
- ¾ teaspoon Table salt (optional)
- 570g Boneless country-style pork ribs, cut into 3.75cm (1½-inch) chunks
- Vegetable oil spray

Directions:
1. Preheat your air fryer to 190°C (375°F).
2. In a large bowl, combine the tapioca flour, chile powder, and salt (if using). Mix until these dry ingredients are well combined.
3. Add the chunks of boneless country-style pork ribs to the bowl with the dry mixture. Toss the pork chunks thoroughly to ensure they are evenly coated.
4. Once the air fryer reaches the desired temperature, gently shake off any excess tapioca coating from the pork chunks.
5. Generously coat the pork chunks on all sides with vegetable oil spray to help achieve extra crispiness.
6. Arrange the coated pork chunks in the air fryer basket in a single layer, though they may touch each other.
7. Air-fry the pork chunks at 190°C (375°F) for 30 minutes, making sure to rearrange the pieces at the 10- and 20-minute marks to expose any parts that may be touching. This will help ensure that they become very crisp and well browned.
8. Once the pork riblets are done cooking, gently pour the contents of the air fryer basket onto a wire rack.
9. Allow the riblets to cool for about 5 minutes before serving.

Greek Pita Pockets

Servings: 4
Cooking Time: 7 Minutes
Ingredients:
- Dressing
- 240ml plain yogurt
- 15ml lemon juice
- 5ml dried dill weed, crushed
- 5ml ground oregano
- 2.5ml salt
- Meatballs
- 225g ground lamb
- 15ml diced onion
- 5ml dried parsley
- 5ml dried dill weed, crushed
- 1.25ml oregano
- 1.25ml coriander
- 1.25ml ground cumin
- 1.25ml salt
- 4 pita halves
- Suggested Toppings:
- Red onion, slivered
- Seedless cucumber, thinly sliced
- Crumbled Feta cheese
- Sliced black olives
- Chopped fresh peppers

Directions:
1. Stir together the dressing ingredients and refrigerate while preparing the lamb.
2. In a large bowl, combine all the meatball ingredients and stir to distribute the seasonings.
3. Shape the meat mixture into 12 small meatballs, rounded or slightly flattened, as preferred.
4. Cook at 200°C (390°F) for 7 minutes or until well done. Remove and drain on paper towels.
5. To serve, pile the meatballs and your choice of toppings into the pita pockets and drizzle with the dressing.

Garlic-buttered Rib Eye Steak

Servings: 2
Cooking Time: 25 Minutes
Ingredients:
- 450g rib eye steak
- Salt and pepper to taste
- 15g butter
- 5g paprika
- 15g chopped rosemary

- 2 garlic cloves, minced
- 30g chopped parsley
- 15g chopped mint

Directions:
1. Preheat your air fryer to 200°C (400°F).
2. Season both sides of the rib eye steak with salt and pepper.
3. Place the seasoned rib eye steak in the greased air fryer basket.
4. Top the steak with butter, minced garlic, paprika, chopped rosemary, and chopped mint.
5. Air fry for 6 minutes, then flip the steak and air fry for an additional 6 minutes. For a medium-rare steak, the internal temperature should reach 60°C (140°F).
6. Remove the steak from the air fryer and let it rest for 5 minutes.
7. Sprinkle the cooked steak with chopped parsley.
8. Slice the steak and serve immediately. Enjoy your Garlic-Buttered Rib Eye Steak!

Beef Al Carbon (street Taco Meat)

Servings: 6
Cooking Time: 8 Minutes
Ingredients:
- 680 grams sirloin steak, cut into 1.3 cm cubes
- 180 ml lime juice
- 120 ml extra-virgin olive oil
- 1 teaspoon ground cumin
- 2 teaspoons garlic powder
- 1 teaspoon salt

Directions:
1. In a large bowl, toss together the sirloin steak cubes, lime juice, olive oil, ground cumin, garlic powder, and salt. Allow the meat to marinate for 30 minutes. Drain off all the marinade and pat the meat dry with paper towels.
2. Preheat the air fryer to 200°C (400°F).
3. Place the marinated meat in the air fryer basket and spray it with cooking spray.
4. Cook the meat for 5 minutes, then toss the meat to ensure even cooking.
5. Continue cooking for another 3 minutes, or until the meat is slightly crispy.

Chicken Fried Steak

Servings: 4
Cooking Time: 15 Minutes
Ingredients:
- 2 eggs
- 120ml buttermilk
- 180g flour
- 3.75ml salt
- 1.25ml pepper
- 450g beef cube steaks
- Salt and pepper to taste
- Oil for misting or cooking spray

Directions:
1. Beat together the eggs and buttermilk in a shallow dish.
2. In another shallow dish, stir together the flour, 3.75ml (¾ teaspoon) salt, and 1.25ml (¼ teaspoon) pepper.
3. Season the cube steaks with salt and pepper to taste.
4. Dip each cube steak in the flour mixture, then the buttermilk and egg wash, and finally the flour mixture again, ensuring they are coated evenly.
5. Spray both sides of the steaks with oil or cooking spray.
6. Cooking in 2 batches, place the steaks in the air fryer basket in a single layer.
7. Cook at 180°C (360°F) for 10 minutes.
8. Spray the tops of the steaks with oil and continue to cook for an additional 5 minutes or until the meat is well done.
9. Repeat the process to cook the remaining steaks.

Balsamic London Broil

Servings: 4
Cooking Time: 25 Minutes
Ingredients:
- 1.13 kilograms top round London broil steak
- 60 ml coconut aminos
- 15 ml balsamic vinegar
- 15 ml olive oil
- 15 ml mustard
- 10 ml maple syrup
- 2 garlic cloves, minced
- 5 grams dried oregano
- Salt and pepper to taste
- 0.6 grams smoked paprika
- 30 grams red onions, chopped

Directions:
1. Whisk together the coconut aminos, mustard, balsamic vinegar, olive oil, maple syrup, minced garlic, dried oregano, chopped red onions, salt, pepper, and smoked paprika in a small bowl to make the marinade.
2. Place the London broil steak in a shallow container and pour the marinade over the steak. Make sure the steak is well coated with the marinade. Cover the container and let it sit for 20 minutes to marinate.
3. Preheat the air fryer to 200°C (400°F).
4. Transfer the marinated steak to the air fryer basket.

5. Air fry for 5 minutes, then flip the steak and air fry for another 4 to 6 minutes, or until the desired level of doneness is reached. Cooking times may vary depending on your air fryer and the thickness of the steak.
6. Allow the cooked steak to rest for 5 minutes before slicing.
7. Serve your Balsamic London Broil warm and enjoy!

Delicious Juicy Pork Meatballs

Servings: 4
Cooking Time: 35 Minutes
Ingredients:
- 30g grated cheddar cheese
- 450g ground pork
- 1 egg
- 15ml Greek yogurt
- 1/2 tsp onion powder
- 60ml chopped parsley
- 30g bread crumbs
- 1/4 tsp garlic powder
- Salt and pepper to taste

Directions:
1. Preheat your air fryer to 180°C (350°F).
2. In a large mixing bowl, combine the ground pork, grated cheddar cheese, egg, Greek yogurt, onion powder, chopped parsley, bread crumbs, garlic powder, salt, and pepper. Mix the ingredients thoroughly until well combined.
3. Form the mixture into 16 equally-sized meatballs.
4. Lightly grease the frying basket of your air fryer.
5. Place the meatballs in the greased frying basket of the air fryer.
6. Air fry the meatballs for 8-10 minutes, flipping them once during the cooking process to ensure even browning.
7. Once the meatballs are cooked through and have a nice browned exterior, remove them from the air fryer.
8. Serve your Delicious Juicy Pork Meatballs while they're still hot and enjoy!

California Burritos

Servings: 4
Cooking Time: 17 Minutes
Ingredients:
- 450g sirloin steak, sliced thin
- 5ml dried oregano
- 5ml ground cumin
- 2.5ml garlic powder
- 16 tater tots
- 80ml sour cream
- ½ lime, juiced
- 30ml hot sauce
- 1 large avocado, pitted
- 5ml salt, divided
- 4 large (20- to 25-centimeter) flour tortillas
- 125g shredded cheddar cheese or Monterey jack
- 30ml avocado oil

Directions:
1. Preheat the air fryer to 190°C (380°F).
2. Season the steak with oregano, cumin, and garlic powder.
3. Place the seasoned steak on one side of the air fryer basket and arrange the tater tots on the other side. It's okay if they touch since the flavors will combine in the burrito. Cook for 8 minutes, toss, and then cook an additional 4 to 6 minutes.
4. In a small bowl, stir together the sour cream, lime juice, and hot sauce.
5. In another small bowl, mash the avocado and season it with 2.5ml (½ teaspoon) of salt, or to taste.
6. To assemble the burrito, lay out the tortillas and equally distribute the cooked steak among them. Season the steak equally with the remaining 2.5ml (½ teaspoon) of salt. Layer the mashed avocado and sour cream mixture on top. Top each tortilla with 4 tater tots and finish with 30g of cheese on each. Roll up the sides and, while holding in the sides, roll up the burrito.
7. Place the burritos in the air fryer basket and brush them with avocado oil. Work in batches if needed.
8. Air fry for 3 minutes or until the burritos are lightly golden on the outside.

Glazed Meatloaf

Servings: 4
Cooking Time: 35-55 Minutes
Ingredients:
- 65g Seasoned Italian-style panko bread crumbs (gluten-free, if a concern)
- 60ml Whole or low-fat milk
- 450g Lean ground beef
- 450g Bulk mild Italian sausage meat (gluten-free, if a concern)
- 1 Large egg(s), well beaten
- 1 teaspoon Dried thyme
- 1 teaspoon Onion powder
- 1 teaspoon Garlic powder
- Vegetable oil spray
- 15ml Ketchup (gluten-free, if a concern)
- 15ml Hoisin sauce (gluten-free, if a concern)

- 10ml Pickle brine, preferably from a jar of jalapeño rings (gluten-free, if a concern)

Directions:
1. Pour the bread crumbs into a large bowl, add the milk, stir gently, and soak for 10 minutes.
2. Preheat the air fryer to 175°C (350°F).
3. Add the ground beef, Italian sausage meat, egg(s), thyme, onion powder, and garlic powder to the bowl with the bread crumbs. Blend gently until well combined. (Clean, dry hands work best!) Form this mixture into an oval loaf about 5cm tall (its length will vary depending on the amount of ingredients) but with a flat bottom. Generously coat the top, bottom, and all sides of the loaf with vegetable oil spray.
4. Use a large, nonstick-safe spatula or perhaps silicone baking mitts to transfer the loaf to the basket. Air-fry undisturbed for 30 minutes for a small meatloaf, 40 minutes for a medium one, or 50 minutes for a large, until an instant-read meat thermometer inserted into the center of the loaf registers 74°C (165°F).
5. Whisk the ketchup, hoisin, and pickle brine in a small bowl until smooth. Brush this over the top and sides of the meatloaf and continue air-frying undisturbed for 5 minutes, or until the glaze has browned a bit.
6. Use that same spatula or those same baking mitts to transfer the meatloaf to a cutting board. Cool for 10 minutes before slicing.

Honey Mustard Pork Roast

Servings: 4
Cooking Time: 50 Minutes
Ingredients:
- 1 boneless pork loin roast
- 2 tablespoons Dijon mustard
- 2 teaspoons olive oil
- 1 teaspoon honey
- 1 garlic clove, minced
- Salt and pepper to taste
- 1 teaspoon dried rosemary

Directions:
1. Preheat your air fryer to 175°C (350°F).
2. In a bowl, whisk together the Dijon mustard, olive oil, honey, minced garlic, salt, pepper, and dried rosemary to create the honey mustard marinade.
3. Massage the honey mustard marinade into the boneless pork loin roast, making sure it covers all sides of the roast.
4. Place the marinated pork loin roast into the air fryer basket.
5. Roast the pork for 40 minutes, turning it over once during cooking to ensure even browning.
6. After roasting, remove the pork loin from the air fryer and let it rest on a cutting board for 5 minutes. This resting period allows the juices to redistribute, resulting in juicier meat.
7. Slice the roasted pork loin into serving portions and serve.

Easy Tex-mex Chimichangas

Servings: 2
Cooking Time: 8 Minutes
Ingredients:
- 115g Thinly sliced deli roast beef, chopped
- 55g Shredded Cheddar cheese or shredded Tex-Mex cheese blend (about 55g)
- 60ml Jarred salsa verde or salsa rojo
- ½ teaspoon Ground cumin
- ½ teaspoon Dried oregano
- 2 Burrito-size (30cm) flour tortilla(s), not corn tortillas (gluten-free, if a concern)
- 160g Canned refried beans
- Vegetable oil spray

Directions:
1. Preheat your air fryer to 190°C (375°F).
2. In a bowl, combine the chopped roast beef, shredded cheese, salsa, ground cumin, and dried oregano. Stir well until all the ingredients are thoroughly mixed.
3. Lay a tortilla on a clean, dry work surface. Spread 80ml (about 1/3 cup) of the refried beans in the center of the lower third of the tortilla, leaving about 2.5cm (1 inch) of space on either side of the spread beans.
4. For one chimichanga, spread all of the roast beef mixture on top of the beans. For two chimichangas, spread half of the roast beef mixture on each tortilla.
5. At either end of the filling mixture, fold the sides of the tortilla up and over the filling, partially covering it. Starting with the unfolded side of the tortilla just below the filling, roll the tortilla closed. Repeat this process for the second filled tortilla, as necessary.
6. Coat the exterior of the tortillas with vegetable oil spray. Place the chimichangas seam side down in the air fryer basket, ensuring there is at least 1.25cm (1/2 inch) of air space between them if you are making two at once.
7. Air-fry the chimichangas for 8 minutes, or until the tortilla is lightly browned and crisp.
8. Using kitchen tongs, gently transfer the chimichangas to a wire rack. Allow them to cool for at least 5 minutes or up to 20 minutes before serving.

Boneless Ribeye Steaks

Servings: 2
Cooking Time: 10-15 Minutes
Ingredients:
- 2 boneless ribeye steaks, approximately 227 grams (8 ounces) each
- 4 teaspoons Worcestershire sauce
- 1/2 teaspoon garlic powder
- Coarsely ground black pepper to taste
- 4 teaspoons extra virgin olive oil
- Salt to taste

Directions:
1. Season both sides of the ribeye steaks with Worcestershire sauce. Use the back of a spoon to spread it evenly.
2. Sprinkle both sides of the steaks with garlic powder and coarsely ground black pepper to taste.
3. Drizzle both sides of the steaks with olive oil, again using the back of a spoon to spread it evenly over the surfaces.
4. Allow the steaks to marinate for 30 minutes.
5. Place both steaks in the air fryer basket and cook at 200°C (390°F) for 5 minutes.
6. Turn the steaks over and cook until done:
7. Medium Rare: Additional 5 minutes
8. Medium: Additional 7 minutes
9. Well Done: Additional 10 minutes
10. Remove the steaks from the air fryer basket and let them sit for 5 minutes. Salt to taste and serve.

Bacon-wrapped Filets Mignons

Servings: 4
Cooking Time: 18 Minutes
Ingredients:
- 4 slices bacon (not thick cut)
- 4 (227-gram) filets mignons
- 1 tablespoon fresh thyme leaves
- Salt and freshly ground black pepper

Directions:
1. Preheat the air fryer to 200°C (400°F).
2. Lay the bacon slices down on a cutting board and sprinkle the thyme leaves on the bacon slices.
3. Remove any string tying the filets and place the steaks down on their sides on top of the bacon slices.
4. Roll the bacon around the side of the filets and secure the bacon to the fillets with a toothpick or two.
5. Season the steaks generously with salt and freshly ground black pepper.
6. Transfer the seasoned steaks to the air fryer.
7. Air-fry for 18 minutes, turning the steaks over halfway through the cooking process. This should cook your steaks to about medium, depending on their thickness.
8. If you prefer your steaks medium-rare or medium-well, simply add or subtract two minutes from the cooking time.
9. Remove the steaks from the air fryer and let them rest for 5 minutes before removing the toothpicks and serving.
10. Enjoy your Bacon-Wrapped Filets Mignons with your preferred sides!

Aromatic Pork Tenderloin

Servings: 6
Cooking Time: 65 Minutes
Ingredients:
- 1 pork tenderloin (about 600 grams)
- 2 tbsp olive oil
- 2 garlic cloves, minced
- 1 tsp dried sage
- 1 tsp dried marjoram
- 1 tsp dried thyme
- 1 tsp paprika
- Salt and pepper to taste

Directions:
1. Preheat the air fryer to 180°C (360°F).
2. Drizzle olive oil over the pork tenderloin and rub minced garlic, dried sage, dried marjoram, dried thyme, paprika, salt, and pepper all over the meat.
3. Place the seasoned tenderloin in the greased air fryer basket.
4. Air fry at 180°C (360°F) for 45 minutes.
5. Flip the pork tenderloin and continue air frying for an additional 15 minutes.
6. Check the temperature for doneness; it should reach at least 70°C (160°F).
7. Allow the cooked tenderloin to rest for 10 minutes before slicing.
8. Serve and enjoy your Aromatic Pork Tenderloin!

Homemade Pork Gyoza

Servings: 4
Cooking Time: 50 Minutes
Ingredients:
- 8 wonton wrappers
- 115g ground pork, browned
- 1 green apple
- 5ml rice vinegar
- 15ml vegetable oil
- 7.5ml oyster sauce
- 15ml soy sauce
- A pinch of white pepper

Directions:
1. Preheat your air fryer to 180°C (350°F).
2. In a small bowl, combine the oyster sauce, soy sauce, rice vinegar, and a pinch of white pepper. Add the browned ground pork and mix thoroughly.
3. Peel and core the green apple, then slice it into small cubes. Add the apple cubes to the pork mixture and combine well.
4. Lay out the wonton wrappers and place a portion of the pork and apple filling in the center of each wrapper.
5. Moisten the edges of the wrappers with a bit of water and fold them into triangles, pressing the edges to seal.
6. Brush the sealed gyoza with vegetable oil to help them crisp up.
7. Place the gyoza in the air fryer basket in a single layer, making sure they do not touch each other.
8. Air fry for about 25 minutes until the gyoza turn crispy golden brown on the outside and are cooked through.
9. Serve your homemade pork gyoza hot with your favorite dipping sauce, and enjoy the delicious flavors!

Barbecue Country-style Pork Ribs

Servings: 3
Cooking Time: 30 Minutes
Ingredients:
- 3 225g boneless country-style pork ribs
- 1½ teaspoons Mild smoked paprika
- 1½ teaspoons Light brown sugar
- ¾ teaspoon Onion powder
- ¾ teaspoon Ground black pepper
- ¼ teaspoon Table salt
- Vegetable oil spray

Directions:
1. Preheat the air fryer to 180°C (350°F). Place the ribs in a bowl on the countertop as the machine heats up.
2. In a small bowl, mix the smoked paprika, brown sugar, onion powder, pepper, and salt until well combined. Rub this mixture over all the surfaces of the country-style ribs. Generously coat the country-style ribs with vegetable oil spray.
3. Arrange the ribs in the air fryer basket with as much air space between them as possible. Air-fry undisturbed for 30 minutes, or until they are browned, sizzling, and an instant-read meat thermometer inserted into one rib registers at least 63°C (145°F).
4. Using kitchen tongs, transfer the country-style ribs to a wire rack. Allow them to cool for 5 minutes before serving.

Baby Back Ribs

Servings: 4
Cooking Time: 36 Minutes
Ingredients:
- 1.02 kilograms Pork baby back rib rack(s)
- 1 tablespoon Dried barbecue seasoning blend or rub (gluten-free, if a concern)
- 240 ml Water
- 3 tablespoons Purchased smooth barbecue sauce (gluten-free, if a concern)

Directions:
1. Preheat the air fryer to 175°C (350°F).
2. Cut the rib rack(s) into 4- to 5-bone sections. You should have about two sections for a small batch, three for a medium batch, and four for a large batch.
3. Sprinkle both sides of these rib sections with the barbecue seasoning blend.
4. Pour the water into the bottom of the air fryer drawer or into a tray placed under the rack. Ensure that the rack is not sitting directly in the water; adjust the water amount according to your machine's instructions.
5. Place the rib sections in the air fryer basket, making sure they are not touching.
6. Air fry for 30 minutes, turning the rib sections once during cooking.
7. If you're using a tray with water, check it a couple of times to ensure it still has water or hasn't overflowed from the rendered fat.
8. Brush half of the barbecue sauce on the exposed side of the rib sections. Air fry undisturbed for 3 minutes.
9. Turn the rib sections over (make sure they're still not touching), brush with the remaining sauce, and air fry undisturbed for 3 more minutes or until sizzling and brown.
10. Use kitchen tongs to transfer the rib sections to a cutting board. Let them stand for 5 minutes, then slice between the bones to serve.

Beef & Spinach Sauté

Servings: 4
Cooking Time: 30 Minutes
Ingredients:
- 2 tomatoes, chopped
- 2 tablespoons crumbled Goat cheese
- 225g ground beef
- 1 shallot, chopped
- 2 garlic cloves, minced
- 2 cups baby spinach
- 2 tablespoons lemon juice
- 80ml beef broth

Directions:
1. Preheat the air fryer to 190°C (370°F).
2. Crumble the ground beef in a baking pan and place it in the air fryer. Air fry for 3-7 minutes, stirring once to ensure even cooking. Drain the meat and make sure it's browned.
3. Toss in the chopped tomatoes, shallot, and minced garlic, and air fry for an additional 4-8 minutes until they become soft.
4. Add the baby spinach, lemon juice, and beef broth to the mixture, and cook for 2-4 minutes until the spinach wilts and everything is well combined.
5. Top the Beef & Spinach Sauté with crumbled goat cheese and serve.

Fish And Seafood Recipes

Filled Mushrooms With Crab & Cheese

Servings: 6
Cooking Time: 30 Minutes
Ingredients:
- 450 grams baby bella mushrooms, stems removed
- 115 grams lump crabmeat, shells discarded
- 55 grams feta cheese, crumbled
- 5 ml prepared horseradish
- 5 ml lemon juice
- Salt and pepper to taste
- 30 grams bread crumbs
- 30 grams butter, melted
- 15 grams chopped dill

Directions:
1. Preheat the air fryer to 175°C (350°F).
2. In a bowl, combine the crumbled feta cheese, lump crabmeat, prepared horseradish, lemon juice, and season with salt and pepper to taste.
3. Evenly stuff the mushroom caps with the crab and cheese mixture.
4. Scatter the bread crumbs over the stuffed mushrooms, and drizzle the melted butter over the breadcrumbs.
5. Place the stuffed mushrooms in the frying basket of the air fryer.
6. Air fry for 10 minutes, or until the mushrooms are cooked and the breadcrumbs are golden brown.
7. Scatter the chopped dill over the stuffed mushrooms before serving.

Dilly Red Snapper

Servings: 4
Cooking Time: 40 Minutes
Ingredients:
- Salt and pepper to taste
- 1/2 tsp ground cumin
- 1/4 tsp cayenne pepper
- 1/4 tsp paprika
- 1 whole red snapper
- 30 grams butter
- 2 garlic cloves, minced
- 15 grams dill
- 4 lemon wedges

Directions:
1. Preheat the air fryer to 180°C (360°F).
2. In a bowl, combine salt, pepper, ground cumin, paprika, and cayenne pepper.

3. Brush the red snapper with butter, then rub it with the seasoning mixture.
4. Stuff the minced garlic and dill inside the cavity of the fish.
5. Place the red snapper into the basket of the air fryer.
6. Roast for 20 minutes, then flip the snapper over and roast for an additional 15 minutes or until the fish is cooked through and has a golden brown exterior.
7. Serve the Dilly Red Snapper with lemon wedges.

Herb-rubbed Salmon With Avocado

Servings: 4
Cooking Time: 30 Minutes
Ingredients:
- 15 milliliters sweet paprika
- 2.5 milliliters cayenne pepper
- 5 milliliters garlic powder
- 5 milliliters dried oregano
- 2.5 milliliters dried coriander
- 5 milliliters dried thyme
- 2.5 milliliters dried dill
- Salt and pepper to taste
- 4 wild salmon fillets
- 30 milliliters chopped red onion
- 22.5 milliliters fresh lemon juice
- 5 milliliters olive oil
- 30 milliliters cilantro, chopped
- 1 avocado, diced

Directions:
1. In a small bowl, mix together the sweet paprika, cayenne pepper, garlic powder, dried oregano, dried thyme, dried dill, dried coriander, salt, and pepper.
2. Spray both sides of the salmon fillets with cooking oil and rub the spice mixture onto the fillets.
3. In a separate bowl, combine the chopped red onion, fresh lemon juice, olive oil, cilantro, salt, and pepper. Allow it to sit for 5 minutes, then gently fold in the diced avocado.
4. Preheat the air fryer to 200°C (400°F).
5. Place the salmon fillets skin-side down in the greased air fryer basket.
6. Air fry for 5-7 minutes or until the fish flakes easily with a fork.
7. Transfer the salmon to a plate and top with the avocado salsa.

Firecracker Popcorn Shrimp

Servings: 6
Cooking Time: 8 Minutes
Ingredients:
- 120 grams all-purpose flour
- 10 ml ground paprika
- 5 ml garlic powder
- 2.5 ml black pepper
- 1.25 ml salt
- 2 eggs, whisked
- 360 ml panko breadcrumbs
- 450 grams small shrimp, peeled and deveined

Directions:
1. Preheat the air fryer to 180°C (360°F).
2. In a medium bowl, place the flour and mix in the paprika, garlic powder, black pepper, and salt.
3. In a shallow dish, place the whisked eggs.
4. In a third dish, place the panko breadcrumbs.
5. Assemble the shrimp by covering them in the flour mixture, then dipping them into the egg, and finally coating them with the breadcrumbs. Repeat until all the shrimp are covered in the breading.
6. Liberally spray the metal trivet that fits in the air fryer basket with olive oil mist. Place the shrimp onto the trivet, leaving space between the shrimp to flip.
7. Cook for 4 minutes, flip the shrimp, and cook for an additional 4 minutes, or until the shrimp are golden brown and cooked through. Repeat until all the shrimp are cooked.
8. Serve the Firecracker Popcorn Shrimp warm with your desired dipping sauce.

Halibut With Coleslaw

Servings: 4
Cooking Time: 30 Minutes
Ingredients:
- 1 bag coleslaw mix
- 60 milliliters mayonnaise
- 5 milliliters lemon zest
- 15 milliliters lemon juice
- 1 shredded carrot
- 120 milliliters buttermilk
- 5 milliliters grated onion
- 4 halibut fillets
- Salt and pepper to taste

Directions:
1. In a bowl, combine the coleslaw mix, mayonnaise, shredded carrot, buttermilk, grated onion, lemon zest, lemon juice, and season with salt to taste. Cover the coleslaw and refrigerate until ready to use.
2. Preheat the air fryer to 180°C (350°F).
3. Sprinkle the halibut fillets with salt and pepper.
4. Grease the air fryer basket, then place the seasoned halibut fillets in it.

5. Air fry for 10 minutes, or until the fillets are opaque and flake easily with a fork.
6. Serve the cooked halibut with the chilled coleslaw.

Malaysian Shrimp With Sambal Mayo

Servings: 4
Cooking Time: 30 Minutes
Ingredients:
- 24 jumbo shrimp, peeled and deveined
- 150 grams panko breadcrumbs
- 3 tablespoons mayonnaise
- 1 tablespoon sambal oelek paste
- 60 grams shredded coconut
- 1 lime, zested
- 1/2 teaspoon ground coriander
- Salt to taste
- 30 grams all-purpose flour
- 2 eggs

Directions:
1. In a bowl, mix together mayonnaise and sambal oelek. Set aside.
2. In another bowl, combine shredded coconut, lime zest, ground coriander, panko breadcrumbs, and salt.
3. In a shallow bowl, place the all-purpose flour. In another shallow bowl, whisk the eggs until well blended.
4. Season the shrimp with salt. Dip each shrimp into the flour, shaking off the excess. Then dip it into the beaten eggs, allowing any excess to drip off. Finally, coat the shrimp with the coconut and panko breadcrumb mixture, pressing gently to adhere.
5. Preheat the air fryer to 180°C (360°F).
6. Place the coated shrimp in the greased frying basket of the air fryer. Cook for 8 minutes, flipping the shrimp once during cooking, until the crust is golden brown and the shrimp is cooked through.
7. Serve the Malaysian shrimp alongside the sambal mayo for dipping.

Herby Prawn & Zucchini Bake

Servings: 4
Cooking Time: 30 Minutes
Ingredients:
- 570 grams prawns, peeled and deveined
- 2 zucchini, sliced
- 30 grams butter, melted
- 2.5 milliliters garlic salt
- 7.5 milliliters dried oregano
- 1 pinch red pepper flakes
- ½ lemon, juiced
- 15 milliliters chopped mint
- 15 milliliters chopped dill

Directions:
1. Preheat the air fryer to 180°C (350°F).
2. In a large bowl, combine the prawns, sliced zucchini, melted butter, garlic salt, dried oregano, and red pepper flakes. Toss to coat evenly.
3. Place the prawns and zucchini in the greased air fryer basket.
4. Air fry for about 6-8 minutes, shaking the basket once during cooking, until the zucchini is golden and the prawns are cooked.
5. Remove the prawns to a serving plate and cover with foil to keep them warm.
6. Serve the hot prawns and zucchini, topped with lemon juice, chopped mint, and chopped dill.

Horseradish Tuna Croquettes

Servings: 4
Cooking Time: 40 Minutes
Ingredients:
- 1 can tuna in water, drained
- 80 milliliters mayonnaise
- 15 milliliters minced celery
- 1 green onion, sliced
- 10 milliliters dried dill
- 5 milliliters lime juice
- 240 milliliters bread crumbs
- 1 egg
- 5 milliliters prepared horseradish

Directions:
1. Preheat the air fryer to 190°C (370°F).
2. In a bowl, combine the drained tuna, mayonnaise, minced celery, sliced green onion, dried dill, lime juice, 60 milliliters (1/4 cup) of bread crumbs, egg, and prepared horseradish. Mix until well combined.
3. Mold the mixture into 12 rectangular mound shapes.
4. Roll each croquette in a shallow dish containing the remaining 180 milliliters (3/4 cup) of bread crumbs, coating them evenly.
5. Lightly grease the air fryer basket.
6. Place the croquettes in the greased basket and air fry for 12 minutes, turning them to cook on all sides until they are golden brown and cooked through.
7. Serve the horseradish tuna croquettes hot.

Cheese & Crab Stuffed Mushrooms

Servings: 2
Cooking Time: 30 Minutes
Ingredients:
- 170g lump crabmeat, shells discarded
- 170g mascarpone cheese, softened
- 2 jalapeño peppers, minced
- 30g diced red onions
- 10g grated Parmesan cheese
- 2 portobello mushroom caps
- 30g butter, divided
- 2.5ml prepared horseradish
- 1.25ml Worcestershire sauce
- 1.25ml smoked paprika
- Salt and pepper to taste
- 30g bread crumbs

Directions:
1. Melt 15g (1 tablespoon) of butter in a skillet over medium heat for 30 seconds. Add in the diced onions and cook for 3 minutes until they become tender.
2. Stir in the mascarpone cheese, Parmesan cheese, horseradish, minced jalapeño peppers, Worcestershire sauce, smoked paprika, salt, and pepper. Cook for 2 minutes until the mixture becomes smooth.
3. Gently fold in the lump crabmeat into the cheese mixture.
4. Spoon the crab and cheese mixture into the portobello mushroom caps. Set aside.
5. Preheat your air fryer to 180°C (350°F).
6. Microwave the remaining butter until melted, then stir in the bread crumbs.
7. Scatter the buttered bread crumbs over the stuffed mushrooms.
8. Place the stuffed mushrooms in the greased air fryer basket.
9. Air fry for 8 minutes until the mushrooms are cooked and the breadcrumbs are crispy.
10. Serve your Cheese & Crab Stuffed Mushrooms immediately.

Lime Bay Scallops

Servings: 4
Cooking Time: 10 Minutes
Ingredients:
- 30 milliliters butter, melted
- 1 lime, juiced
- 1.25 milliliters salt
- 450 grams bay scallops
- 30 milliliters chopped cilantro

Directions:
1. Preheat the air fryer to 180°C (350°F).
2. In a bowl, combine all the ingredients except for the cilantro.
3. Place the bay scallops in the air fryer basket.
4. Air fry for 5 minutes, tossing them once during cooking.
5. Serve the Lime Bay Scallops immediately, topped with chopped cilantro.

Almond Topped Trout

Servings: 4
Cooking Time: 20 Minutes
Ingredients:
- 4 trout fillets
- 30ml olive oil
- Salt and pepper to taste
- 2 garlic cloves, sliced
- 1 lemon, sliced
- 15g flaked almonds

Directions:
1. Preheat the air fryer to 190°C (375°F).
2. Lightly brush each fillet with olive oil on both sides and season with salt and pepper.
3. Place the fillets in a single layer in the frying basket.
4. Place the sliced garlic over the tops of the trout fillets, then top with lemon slices.
5. Cook for 12-15 minutes in the preheated air fryer.
6. Serve the trout fillets topped with flaked almonds.
7. Enjoy your Almond Topped Trout!

Flounder Fillets

Servings: 4
Cooking Time: 8 Minutes
Ingredients:
- 1 egg white
- 15 ml water
- 120 grams panko breadcrumbs
- 30 ml extra-light virgin olive oil
- 4 113-gram flounder fillets
- Salt and pepper
- Oil for misting or cooking spray

Directions:
1. Preheat the air fryer to 199°C (390°F).
2. Beat together the egg white and water in a shallow dish.
3. In another shallow dish, mix the panko breadcrumbs and olive oil until well combined and crumbly (best done by hand).
4. Season the flounder fillets with salt and pepper to taste.

5. Dip each fillet into the egg mixture and then roll it in the panko breadcrumbs, pressing the crumbs onto the fish to ensure it is nicely coated.
6. Spray the air fryer basket with nonstick cooking spray and add the fillets.
7. Cook at 199°C (390°F) for 3 minutes.
8. Spray the fish fillets but do not turn them. Cook for an additional 5 minutes or until they are golden brown and crispy.
9. Using a spatula, carefully remove the fish from the basket and serve.

Butternut Squash–wrapped Halibut Fillets

Servings: 3
Cooking Time: 11 Minutes
Ingredients:
- 375g long spiralized peeled and seeded butternut squash strands
- 3 140-170g skinless halibut fillets
- 3 tablespoons butter, melted
- 3/4 teaspoon mild paprika
- 3/4 teaspoon table salt
- 3/4 teaspoon ground black pepper

Directions:
1. Preheat your air fryer to 190°C (375°F).
2. Take 5 long butternut squash strands and wrap them around each halibut fillet, then set them aside. Repeat for any remaining fillets.
3. In a small bowl, mix together the melted butter, paprika, salt, and pepper.
4. Brush the butter and spice mixture over the squash-wrapped fillets, ensuring they are coated on all sides.
5. When your air fryer reaches the desired temperature, place the fillets in the basket with as much space between them as possible.
6. Air-fry the fillets undisturbed for 10 minutes, or until the squash strands have browned but not burned. If your air fryer is set to 180°C (360°F), you may need to add an extra minute to the cooking time. Keep an eye on the fish after the 8-minute mark to prevent overcooking.
7. Gently transfer the cooked fillets to a serving platter or individual plates using a nonstick-safe spatula.
8. Allow them to cool for only a minute or so before serving.

Easy-peasy Shrimp

Servings: 2
Cooking Time: 15 Minutes
Ingredients:
- 450 grams tail-on shrimp, deveined
- 30 ml butter, melted
- 15 ml lemon juice
- 15 ml dill, chopped

Directions:
1. Preheat the air fryer to 175°C (350°F).
2. In a bowl, combine the shrimp and melted butter.
3. Place the shrimp in the greased frying basket of the air fryer.
4. Air fry the shrimp for 6 minutes, flipping them once halfway through the cooking time.
5. Squeeze lemon juice over the cooked shrimp and sprinkle with chopped dill.
6. Serve the Easy-Peasy Shrimp hot.

Catalan-style Crab Samfaina

Servings: 4
Cooking Time: 30 Minutes
Ingredients:
- 1 peeled eggplant, cubed
- 1 zucchini, cubed
- 1 onion, chopped
- 1 red bell pepper, chopped
- 2 large tomatoes, chopped
- 15ml olive oil
- 1/2 tsp dried thyme
- 1/2 tsp dried basil
- Salt and pepper to taste
- 360g cooked crab meat

Directions:
1. Preheat your air fryer to 200°C (400°F).
2. In a pan, mix together all the ingredients except for the crab meat.
3. Place the pan in the air fryer and bake for 9 minutes.
4. Remove the pan from the air fryer and stir in the cooked crab meat.
5. Return the pan to the air fryer and roast for an additional 2-5 minutes until the vegetables are tender, and the crab samfaina is bubbling.
6. Serve your hot Catalan-Style Crab Samfaina.

Horseradish Crusted Salmon

Servings: 2
Cooking Time: 14 Minutes
Ingredients:
- 2 (140-gram) salmon fillets
- Salt and freshly ground black pepper
- 10 milliliters Dijon mustard

- 50 grams panko breadcrumbs*
- 30 milliliters prepared horseradish
- 2.5 milliliters finely chopped lemon zest
- 15 milliliters olive oil
- 15 milliliters chopped fresh parsley

Directions:
1. Preheat the air fryer to 180°C (360°F).
2. Season the salmon fillets with salt and freshly ground black pepper.
3. Spread the Dijon mustard evenly over the surface of the salmon fillets.
4. In a small bowl, combine the panko breadcrumbs, prepared horseradish, finely chopped lemon zest, and olive oil.
5. Spread the breadcrumb mixture over the top of the salmon fillets, pressing down lightly to adhere it to the salmon using the mustard as "glue."
6. Place the salmon fillets in the air fryer basket.
7. Air-fry at 180°C (360°F) for 14 minutes (adjust the time depending on the thickness of your fillets) or until the salmon feels firm to the touch.
8. Sprinkle the cooked salmon with chopped fresh parsley.
9. Serve immediately.

Herb-crusted Sole

Servings: 4
Cooking Time: 20 Minutes
Ingredients:
- ½ lemon, juiced and zested
- 4 sole fillets
- 2.5 milliliters dried thyme
- 2.5 milliliters dried marjoram
- 2.5 milliliters dried parsley
- Black pepper to taste
- 1 bread slice, crumbled
- 10 milliliters olive oil

Directions:
1. Preheat the air fryer to 160°C (320°F).
2. In a bowl, combine the lemon zest, dried thyme, dried marjoram, dried parsley, black pepper, breadcrumbs, and olive oil. Stir until well mixed.
3. Arrange the sole fillets on a lined baking pan, skin-side down.
4. Drizzle the lemon juice over the fillets.
5. Press the fillets firmly into the breadcrumb mixture to coat them evenly.
6. Air fry for 8-11 minutes, or until the breadcrumbs are crisp and golden brown.
7. Serve the herb-crusted sole warm.

King Prawns Al Ajillo

Servings: 4
Cooking Time: 15 Minutes
Ingredients:
- 570 grams peeled king prawns, deveined
- 120 milliliters grated Parmesan
- 15 milliliters olive oil
- 15 milliliters lemon juice
- 2.5 milliliters garlic powder
- 2 garlic cloves, minced

Directions:
1. Preheat the air fryer to 180°C (350°F).
2. In a large bowl, add the king prawns and sprinkle them with olive oil, lemon juice, and garlic powder.
3. Toss in the minced garlic and Parmesan, then toss everything together to coat the prawns evenly.
4. Place the prawns in the air fryer basket.
5. Air fry for 10-15 minutes or until the prawns are cooked through. Shake the basket once while cooking to ensure even cooking.
6. Serve the King Prawns al Ajillo immediately.

Garlic-lemon Steamer Clams

Servings: 2
Cooking Time: 30 Minutes
Ingredients:
- 25 Manila clams, scrubbed
- 30 milliliters butter, melted
- 1 garlic clove, minced
- 2 lemon wedges

Directions:
1. Place the clams in a large bowl filled with water and let them sit for 10 minutes. Drain.
2. Pour more water over the clams and let them sit for an additional 10 minutes. Drain.
3. Preheat the air fryer to 180°C (350°F).
4. Place the clams in the air fryer basket and air fry for 7 minutes.
5. Discard any clams that do not open.
6. Remove the clams from their shells and place them into a large serving dish.
7. Drizzle the melted butter and minced garlic over the clams and squeeze lemon on top.
8. Serve and enjoy your garlic-lemon steamer clams!

Coconut Shrimp Recipes

Servings: 4
Cooking Time: 12 Minutes
Ingredients:
- 450g large shrimp (about 16 to 20), peeled and deveined
- 120g flour
- Salt and freshly ground black pepper
- 2 egg whites
- 120g fine breadcrumbs
- 120g shredded unsweetened coconut
- Zest of one lime
- 2.5ml salt
- 0.3 to 0.6ml ground cayenne pepper
- Vegetable or canola oil
- Sweet chili sauce or duck sauce (for serving)

Directions:
1. Set up a dredging station. Place the flour in a shallow dish and season it well with salt and freshly ground black pepper. Whisk the egg whites in a second shallow dish. In a third shallow dish, combine the breadcrumbs, shredded coconut, lime zest, salt, and ground cayenne pepper.
2. Preheat your air fryer to 200°C (400°F).
3. Dredge each shrimp first in the flour, then dip it in the egg mixture, and finally press it into the breadcrumb-coconut mixture to coat all sides. Place the breaded shrimp on a plate or baking sheet and spray both sides with vegetable oil.
4. Air-fry the shrimp in two batches, being sure not to overcrowd the basket. Air-fry for 5 minutes, turning the shrimp over for the last minute or two. Repeat with the second batch of shrimp.
5. Lower the temperature of the air fryer to 170°C (340°F). Return the first batch of shrimp to the air fryer basket with the second batch and air-fry for an additional 2 minutes, just to reheat everything.
6. Serve with sweet chili sauce, duck sauce, or enjoy them plain!

Crunchy Flounder Gratin

Servings: 4
Cooking Time: 20 Minutes
Ingredients:
- 30 grams grated Parmesan
- 4 flounder fillets
- 4 tbsp butter, melted
- 30 grams panko breadcrumbs
- 1/2 tsp paprika
- 1 egg
- Salt and pepper to taste
- 1/2 tsp dried oregano
- 1/2 tsp dried basil
- 1 tsp dried thyme
- 1 lemon, quartered
- 1 tbsp chopped parsley

Directions:
1. Preheat the air fryer to 190°C (375°F).
2. In a bowl, whisk the egg until smooth.
3. Brush both sides of the flounder fillets with some of the melted butter.
4. In another bowl, combine the remaining melted butter, panko breadcrumbs, Parmesan cheese, salt, paprika, thyme, oregano, basil, and pepper. Mix until the mixture becomes crumbly.
5. Dip each flounder fillet into the beaten egg and then into the breadcrumb mixture, ensuring they are fully coated.
6. Place the coated flounder fillets in the frying basket of the air fryer.
7. Air fry for 5 minutes, then carefully flip the fillets, and air fry for an additional 6 minutes or until they are crispy and golden on the outside.
8. Garnish the cooked flounder with lemon wedges and chopped parsley.
9. Serve hot and enjoy your Crunchy Flounder Gratin!

Chili Blackened Shrimp

Servings: 4
Cooking Time: 15 Minutes
Ingredients:
- 450g peeled shrimp, deveined
- 5g paprika
- 2.5g dried dill
- 2.5g red chili flakes
- 1/2 lemon, juiced
- Salt and pepper to taste

Directions:
1. Preheat your air fryer to 200°C (400°F).
2. In a resealable bag, combine the shrimp, paprika, dried dill, red chili flakes, lemon juice, salt, and pepper.
3. Seal the bag and shake well to coat the shrimp with the seasonings.
4. Place the seasoned shrimp in the greased air fryer basket.
5. Air fry for 7-8 minutes, shaking the basket once during cooking until the shrimp are blackened and cooked through.
6. Allow the shrimp to cool slightly and then serve.

Beer-breaded Halibut Fish Tacos

Servings: 4
Cooking Time: 10 Minutes
Ingredients:
- 450g halibut, cut into 2.5cm strips
- 240ml light beer
- 1 jalapeño, minced and divided
- 1 clove garlic, minced
- 1g ground cumin
- 60g cornmeal
- 30g all-purpose flour
- 6.25g sea salt, divided
- 200g shredded cabbage
- 1 lime, juiced and divided
- 60ml Greek yogurt
- 60ml mayonnaise
- 200g grape tomatoes, quartered
- 30g chopped cilantro
- 60g chopped onion
- 1 egg, whisked
- 8 corn tortillas

Directions:
1. In a shallow baking dish, place the halibut, light beer, 1 teaspoon of minced jalapeño, minced garlic, and ground cumin. Cover and refrigerate for 30 minutes.
2. Meanwhile, in a medium bowl, mix together the cornmeal, flour, and ½ teaspoon of sea salt.
3. In a large bowl, combine the shredded cabbage, 1 tablespoon of lime juice, Greek yogurt, mayonnaise, and ½ teaspoon of sea salt.
4. In a small bowl, make the pico de gallo by mixing together the grape tomatoes, cilantro, chopped onion, ¼ teaspoon of sea salt, the remaining minced jalapeño, and the remaining lime juice.
5. Remove the fish from the refrigerator and discard the marinade. Dredge the fish in the whisked egg; then dredge the fish in the cornmeal flour mixture until all pieces of fish are breaded.
6. Preheat the air fryer to 175°C (350°F).
7. Place the fish in the air fryer basket and spray liberally with cooking spray. Cook for 6 minutes, flip and shake the fish, and cook for another 4 minutes.
8. While the fish is cooking, heat the tortillas in a heavy skillet for 1 to 2 minutes over high heat.
9. To assemble the tacos, place the battered fish on the heated tortillas and top with slaw and pico de gallo. Serve immediately.

Classic Crab Cakes

Servings: 4
Cooking Time: 10 Minutes
Ingredients:
- 280g Lump crabmeat, picked over for shell and cartilage
- 6 tablespoons Plain panko bread crumbs (gluten-free, if a concern)
- 6 tablespoons Chopped drained jarred roasted red peppers
- 4 Medium scallions, trimmed and thinly sliced
- 60ml Regular or low-fat mayonnaise (not fat-free; gluten-free, if a concern)
- 1/4 teaspoon Dried dill
- 1/4 teaspoon Dried thyme
- 1/4 teaspoon Onion powder
- 1/4 teaspoon Table salt
- 1/8 teaspoon Celery seeds
- Up to 1/8 teaspoon Cayenne
- Vegetable oil spray

Directions:
1. Preheat your air fryer to 200°C (400°F).
2. Gently mix the crabmeat, bread crumbs, red pepper, scallion, mayonnaise, dill, thyme, onion powder, salt, celery seeds, and cayenne in a bowl until well combined.
3. Use clean and dry hands to form 120g of this mixture into a tightly packed 2.5cm-thick, 7.5- to 10cm-wide patty. Coat the top and bottom of the patty with vegetable oil spray and set it aside. Continue making 1 more patty for a small batch, 3 more for a medium batch, or 5 more for a larger one, coating them with vegetable oil spray on both sides.
4. Set the patties in one layer in the air fryer basket and air-fry undisturbed for 10 minutes, or until lightly browned and cooked through.
5. Use a nonstick-safe spatula to transfer the crab cakes to a serving platter or plates. Wait a couple of minutes before serving.

Cilantro Sea Bass

Servings: 2
Cooking Time: 15 Minutes
Ingredients:
- Salt and pepper to taste
- 5ml olive oil
- 2 sea bass fillets
- 2.5ml berbere seasoning
- 10ml chopped cilantro
- 5ml dried thyme
- 2.5ml garlic powder

- 4 lemon quarters

Directions:
1. Preheat your air fryer to 190°C (375°F).
2. Rub the sea bass fillets with olive oil, dried thyme, garlic powder, salt, and black pepper. Season with berbere seasoning.
3. Place the seasoned fillets in the greased frying basket of the air fryer.
4. Air Fry for 6-8 minutes until the sea bass fillets are cooked through.
5. Let the cooked sea bass rest for 5 minutes on a serving plate.
6. Scatter chopped cilantro over the sea bass fillets.
7. Serve with lemon quarters on the side.

Lobster Tails With Lemon Garlic Butter

Servings: 2
Cooking Time: 5 Minutes

Ingredients:
- 115 grams unsalted butter
- 15 milliliters finely chopped lemon zest
- 1 clove garlic, thinly sliced
- 2 (170-gram) lobster tails
- Salt and freshly ground black pepper
- 120 milliliters white wine
- ½ lemon, sliced
- Vegetable oil

Directions:
1. Begin by making the lemon garlic butter. In a small saucepan, combine the butter, lemon zest, and garlic. Melt and simmer the butter on the stovetop over the lowest possible heat while you prepare the lobster tails.
2. Prepare the lobster tails by cutting down the middle of the top of the shell. Crack the bottom shell by squeezing the sides of the lobster together to access the lobster meat inside. Pull the lobster tail up out of the shell, leaving it attached at the base of the tail. Lay the lobster meat on top of the shell and season with salt and freshly ground black pepper. Pour a little of the lemon garlic butter on top of the lobster meat and transfer the lobster to the refrigerator so that the butter solidifies a little.
3. Pour the white wine into the air fryer drawer and add the lemon slices. Preheat the air fryer to 200°C (400°F) for 5 minutes.
4. Transfer the lobster tails to the air fryer basket. Air-fry at 190°C (370°F) for 5 minutes, brushing more butter on halfway through cooking. Add a minute or two if your lobster tail is more than 170 grams.
5. Remove and serve the Lobster Tails with Lemon Garlic Butter with more butter for dipping or drizzling.

Blackened Catfish

Servings: 4
Cooking Time: 8 Minutes

Ingredients:
- 1 teaspoon paprika
- 1 teaspoon garlic powder
- 1 teaspoon onion powder
- 1 teaspoon ground dried thyme
- 1/2 teaspoon ground black pepper
- 1/8 teaspoon cayenne pepper
- 1/2 teaspoon dried oregano
- 1/8 teaspoon crushed red pepper flakes
- 450g catfish fillets
- 1/2 teaspoon sea salt
- 2 tablespoons butter, melted
- 1 tablespoon extra-virgin olive oil
- 2 tablespoons chopped parsley
- 1 lemon, cut into wedges

Directions:
1. In a small bowl, combine the paprika, garlic powder, onion powder, thyme, black pepper, cayenne pepper, oregano, and crushed red pepper flakes.
2. Pat the catfish fillets dry with paper towels. Season them with sea salt, and then coat them evenly with the blackening seasoning mixture.
3. In another small bowl, mix together the melted butter and olive oil. Drizzle this mixture over the seasoned catfish fillets, making sure they are fully coated.
4. Preheat your air fryer to 180°C (350°F).
5. Place the seasoned catfish fillets in the air fryer basket and cook for 8 minutes. Check the fish for doneness after 4 minutes; it should flake easily when cooked through.
6. Remove the catfish from the air fryer, top them with chopped parsley, and serve with lemon wedges.

Halibut Quesadillas

Servings: 2
Cooking Time: 30 Minutes

Ingredients:
- 30 grams shredded cheddar
- 30 grams shredded mozzarella
- 5 milliliters olive oil
- 2 tortilla shells
- 1 halibut fillet
- ½ peeled avocado, sliced
- 1 garlic clove, minced

- Salt and pepper to taste
- 2.5 milliliters lemon juice

Directions:
1. Preheat the air fryer to 180°C (350°F).
2. Brush the halibut fillet with olive oil and sprinkle it with salt and pepper.
3. Bake the halibut in the air fryer for 12-14 minutes, flipping it once until it's cooked through.
4. In a bowl, combine the avocado, minced garlic, salt, pepper, and lemon juice. Mash lightly with a fork until the avocado is slightly chunky.
5. Spread the resulting guacamole on one tortilla shell.
6. Top the guacamole with the cooked fish and a mixture of shredded cheddar and mozzarella cheese.
7. Cover with the second tortilla shell.
8. Bake the quesadilla in the air fryer for 6-8 minutes, flipping it once, until the cheese is melted.
9. Serve immediately.

Kid's Flounder Fingers

Servings: 4
Cooking Time: 45 Minutes
Ingredients:
- 450 grams catfish flounder fillets, cut into 2.5-centimeter chunks
- 120 grams seasoned fish fry breading mix

Directions:
1. Preheat the air fryer to 200°C (400°F).
2. In a resealable bag, add the flounder chunks and breading mix.
3. Seal the bag and shake it until the fish is coated evenly.
4. Place the nuggets in the greased air fryer basket.
5. Air fry for 18-20 minutes, shaking the basket once during cooking, until the flounder fingers are crisp.
6. Serve the warm flounder fingers and enjoy!

Home-style Fish Sticks

Servings: 4
Cooking Time: 30 Minutes
Ingredients:
- 450 grams cod fillets, cut into sticks
- 120 grams flour
- 1 egg
- 30 grams cornmeal
- Salt and pepper to taste
- 1 milliliter smoked paprika
- 1 lemon

Directions:
1. Preheat the air fryer to 180°C (350°F).
2. In a bowl, place 120 grams of flour.
3. In another bowl, beat the egg.
4. In a third bowl, combine the remaining flour, cornmeal, salt, black pepper, and smoked paprika.
5. Roll the fish sticks in the flour, shaking off any excess flour.
6. Dip them in the beaten egg, allowing any excess to drip off.
7. Finally, dredge the fish sticks in the cornmeal mixture, pressing lightly to adhere.
8. Place the fish sticks in the greased air fryer basket.
9. Air fry for 10 minutes, flipping them once during cooking until they are golden and crispy.
10. Serve the home-style fish sticks with a squeeze of lemon.

Hazelnut-crusted Fish

Servings: 4
Cooking Time: 30 Minutes
Ingredients:
- 120 grams ground hazelnuts
- 1 scallion, finely chopped
- 1 lemon, juiced and zested
- 7.5 milliliters olive oil
- Salt and pepper to taste
- 3 skinless sea bass fillets
- 5 milliliters Dijon mustard

Directions:
1. In a small bowl, combine the ground hazelnuts, finely chopped scallion, lemon zest, olive oil, and season with salt and pepper. Mix until well combined.
2. Spray only the top of the fish fillets with cooking oil, then squeeze lemon juice onto the fish.
3. Coat the top of each fish fillet with Dijon mustard.
4. Spread the hazelnut mixture over the mustard-coated side of the fish and press gently to ensure it sticks to the fish.
5. Preheat the air fryer to 190°C (375°F).
6. Place the fish fillets in the greased air fryer basket.
7. Air fry for 7-8 minutes or until the hazelnut crust starts to brown, and the fish is cooked through.
8. Serve the hazelnut-crusted fish hot.

Poultry Recipes

Crunchy Chicken Tenders

Servings: 4
Cooking Time: xx
Ingredients:
- 8 regular chicken tenders (frozen work best)
- 1 egg
- 2 tbsp olive oil
- 150g dried breadcrumbs

Directions:
1. Heat the fryer to 175°C
2. In a small bowl, beat the egg
3. In another bowl, combine the oil and the breadcrumbs together
4. Take one tender and first dip it into the egg, and then cover it in the breadcrumb mixture
5. Place the tender into the fryer basket
6. Repeat with the rest of the tenders, arranging them carefully so they don't touch inside the basket
7. Cook for 12 minutes, checking that they are white in the centre before serving

Chicken Cordon Bleu

Servings: 4
Cooking Time: 20 Minutes
Ingredients:
- 4 small boneless, skinless chicken breasts
- Salt and pepper, to taste
- 4 slices of deli ham
- 4 slices of deli Swiss cheese (approximately 7.5 to 10 cm square)
- 2 tablespoons olive oil
- 2 teaspoons dried marjoram
- ¼ teaspoon paprika

Directions:
1. Begin by carefully slicing each chicken breast horizontally, leaving one edge intact.
2. Lay the chicken breasts open flat and season them with salt and pepper to your liking.
3. On top of each chicken breast, place a slice of ham.
4. Cut the cheese slices in half and position one-half on each chicken breast, reserving the remaining halves for later use.
5. Carefully roll up the chicken breasts to enclose the cheese and ham, securing them in place with toothpicks.
6. In a small bowl, combine the olive oil, dried marjoram, and paprika. Mix well and rub this mixture evenly over the outsides of the chicken breasts.
7. Place the prepared chicken in the air fryer basket and cook at 180°C (360°F) for approximately 20 minutes or until the chicken is thoroughly cooked, and the juices run clear.
8. Remove all toothpicks from the chicken breasts. To avoid any burns, transfer the chicken breasts to a plate to remove the toothpicks safely, and then return them immediately to the air fryer basket.
9. Lastly, add half a cheese slice on top of each chicken breast, and cook for an additional minute or until the cheese has melted and is slightly bubbly.

Christmas Chicken & Roasted Grape Salad

Servings: 4
Cooking Time: 40 Minutes
Ingredients:
- 3 chicken breasts, pat-dried
- 1 tsp paprika
- Salt and pepper to taste
- 400g seedless red grapes
- 120ml mayonnaise
- 120ml plain yogurt
- 2 tbsp honey mustard
- 2 tbsp fresh lemon juice
- 100g chopped celery
- 2 scallions, chopped
- 2 tbsp walnuts, chopped

Directions:
1. Preheat the air fryer to 190°C (370°F).
2. Sprinkle the chicken breasts with paprika, salt, and pepper.
3. Transfer the seasoned chicken breasts to the greased air fryer basket and Air Fry for 16-19 minutes, flipping once during cooking. Ensure the chicken is cooked through, with no pink inside. Once done, remove the chicken and set it on a cutting board.
4. Place the grapes in the air fryer basket and spray them with cooking oil. Fry for 4 minutes or until the grapes are hot and tender.
5. In a bowl, mix together the mayonnaise, plain yogurt, honey mustard, and fresh lemon juice. Whisk until well combined.

6. Cube the cooked chicken and add it to the dressing mixture along with the roasted grapes, chopped walnuts, chopped celery, and scallions. Toss gently to coat all the ingredients with the dressing.
7. Serve the Christmas Chicken & Roasted Grape Salad as a delightful holiday dish.

Herb-marinated Chicken

Servings: 4
Cooking Time: 25 Minutes
Ingredients:
- 4 chicken breasts
- 2 tsp rosemary, minced
- 2 tsp thyme, minced
- Salt and pepper to taste
- 120ml chopped cilantro
- 1 lime, juiced

Directions:
1. Place the chicken breasts in a resealable bag.
2. Add the minced rosemary, minced thyme, salt, pepper, chopped cilantro, and lime juice to the bag.
3. Seal the bag and toss to coat the chicken thoroughly. Refrigerate for 2 hours to marinate.
4. Preheat the air fryer to 200°C (400°F).
5. Arrange the marinated chicken breasts in a single layer in the greased frying basket.
6. Lightly spray the chicken with cooking oil.
7. Air fry for 6-7 minutes, then flip the chicken and cook for another 3 minutes or until the chicken is cooked through.
8. Serve your herb-marinated chicken and enjoy!

Chicken Adobo

Servings: 6
Cooking Time: 12 Minutes
Ingredients:
- 6 boneless chicken thighs
- 60ml soy sauce or tamari
- 120ml rice wine vinegar
- 4 cloves garlic, minced
- 0.3ml crushed red pepper flakes
- 2.5ml black pepper

Directions:
1. Place the chicken thighs into a resealable plastic bag with the soy sauce or tamari, rice wine vinegar, minced garlic, and crushed red pepper flakes. Seal the bag and let the chicken marinate in the refrigerator for at least 1 hour.
2. Preheat your air fryer to 200°C (400°F).
3. Drain the chicken and pat it dry with a paper towel. Season the chicken with black pepper and generously spray with cooking spray.
4. Place the chicken in the air fryer basket.
5. Cook the chicken for 9 minutes, then turn it over and check for an internal temperature of 74°C (165°F). Cook for an additional 3 minutes if needed.

Chilean-style Chicken Empanadas

Servings: 4
Cooking Time: 25 Minutes
Ingredients:
- 115g chorizo sausage, casings removed and crumbled
- 15ml olive oil
- 115g chicken breasts, diced
- 30g black olives, sliced
- 5ml chili powder
- 5ml paprika
- 30g raisins
- 4 empanada shells

Directions:
1. Preheat the air fryer to 175°C (350°F).
2. Warm the olive oil in a skillet over medium heat. Sauté the chicken and chorizo, breaking up the chorizo, for 3-4 minutes.
3. Add the raisins, chili powder, paprika, and olives to the skillet. Stir well. Remove the skillet from heat and allow the mixture to cool slightly.
4. Divide the chorizo mixture between the empanada shells and fold them over to cover the filling. Seal the edges with water and press down with a fork to secure.
5. Place the empanadas in the air fryer basket.
6. Bake for 15 minutes, flipping them once during cooking, until they turn golden brown.
7. Serve the Chilean-Style Chicken Empanadas while they are still warm. Enjoy!

Cajun Fried Chicken

Servings: 3
Cooking Time: 35 Minutes
Ingredients:
- 240ml Cajun seasoning
- 2.5ml mango powder
- 6 chicken legs, bone-in

Directions:
1. Preheat your air fryer to 180°C (360°F).
2. Place half of the Cajun seasoning and 180ml (3/4 cup) of water in a bowl and mix well to dissolve any lumps.

3. In a shallow bowl, combine the remaining Cajun seasoning and mango powder, stirring to combine.
4. Dip each chicken leg in the batter mixture, then coat it in the mango seasoning.
5. Lightly spritz the chicken legs with cooking spray to help with browning.
6. Place the coated chicken legs in the air fryer.
7. Air fry the chicken for 14-16 minutes, turning them once during cooking, until the chicken is cooked through, and the coating is brown.
8. Serve and enjoy your Cajun Fried Chicken!

Italian-inspired Chicken Pizzadillas

Servings: 4
Cooking Time: 25 Minutes
Ingredients:
- 400g cooked boneless, skinless chicken, shredded
- 100g grated provolone cheese
- 8 basil and mint leaves, julienned
- 1/2 tsp salt
- 1 tsp garlic powder
- 45g butter, melted
- 8 flour tortillas
- 250ml marinara sauce
- 100g grated cheddar cheese

Directions:
1. Preheat the air fryer to 180°C (350°F).
2. Sprinkle the shredded chicken with salt and garlic powder.
3. Lightly brush one side of a tortilla with melted butter.
4. Spread 60ml (1/4 cup) of marinara sauce onto the buttered side of the tortilla.
5. Top the sauce with 125g (1/2 cup) of shredded chicken, 25g (1/4 cup) of cheddar cheese, 25g (1/4 cup) of provolone cheese, and 25% of the julienned basil and mint leaves.
6. Place another tortilla on top and lightly brush it with butter.
7. Repeat the process with the remaining ingredients to make additional pizzadillas.
8. Place the assembled pizzadillas, butter side down, in the air fryer frying basket.
9. Bake for 3 minutes or until they are golden and crispy.
10. Cut each pizzadilla into 6 sections and serve your Italian-Inspired Chicken Pizzadillas.

Cheesy Chicken Tenders

Servings: 4
Cooking Time: 25 Minutes
Ingredients:
- 240ml grated Parmesan cheese
- 60ml grated cheddar
- 570 grams chicken tenders
- 1 egg, beaten
- 30ml milk
- Salt and pepper to taste
- 2.5ml garlic powder
- 5ml dried thyme
- 1.25ml shallot powder

Directions:
1. Preheat your air fryer to 200°C (400°F).
2. Stir the beaten egg and milk together until combined.
3. On a plate, mix together the salt, pepper, garlic powder, dried thyme, shallot powder, cheddar cheese, and Parmesan cheese.
4. Dip each chicken tender into the egg mixture, then into the cheese mixture, pressing to coat them evenly.
5. Place the coated chicken tenders in the air fryer frying basket in a single layer. If you have a raised rack, you can use it to cook more at one time.
6. Spray all the chicken tenders with oil.
7. Bake the chicken tenders for 12-16 minutes, flipping them once halfway through cooking.
8. Serve your Cheesy Chicken Tenders while hot.

Chicken Souvlaki Gyros

Servings: 4
Cooking Time: 18 Minutes
Ingredients:
- 60ml extra-virgin olive oil
- 1 clove garlic, crushed
- 1 tablespoon Italian seasoning
- ½ teaspoon paprika
- ½ lemon, sliced
- ¼ teaspoon salt
- 450g boneless, skinless chicken breasts
- 4 whole-grain pita breads
- 1 cup shredded lettuce
- ½ cup chopped tomatoes
- ¼ cup chopped red onion
- 60ml cucumber yogurt sauce

Directions:
1. In a large resealable plastic bag, combine the olive oil, garlic, Italian seasoning, paprika, lemon, and salt. Add the chicken to the bag and secure it shut. Vigorously shake until all the ingredients are combined. Set in the fridge for 2 hours to marinate.

2. When ready to cook, preheat the air fryer to 180°C (360°F).
3. Liberally spray the air fryer basket with olive oil mist. Remove the chicken from the bag and discard the leftover marinade. Place the chicken into the air fryer basket, allowing enough room between the chicken breasts to flip.
4. Cook for 10 minutes, flip, and cook for another 8 minutes.
5. Remove the chicken from the air fryer basket when it has cooked (or the internal temperature of the chicken reaches 74°C). Let it rest for 5 minutes. Then thinly slice the chicken into strips.
6. Assemble the gyros by placing the pita bread on a flat surface and topping with chicken, lettuce, tomatoes, onion, and a drizzle of yogurt sauce.
7. Serve warm.

Charred Chicken Breasts

Servings: 2
Cooking Time:xx
Ingredients:
- 2 tsp paprika
- 1 tsp ground thyme
- 1 tsp cumin
- ½ tsp cayenne pepper
- ½ tsp onion powder
- ½ tsp black pepper
- ¼ tsp salt
- 2 tsp vegetable oil
- 2 skinless boneless chicken breasts, cut into halves

Directions:
1. Take a bowl and add the paprika, thyme, cumin, cayenne pepper, onion powder, black pepper and salt
2. Coat each chicken breast with oil and dredge chicken in the spice mixture
3. Preheat air fryer to 175C
4. Cook for 10 minutes and flip
5. Cook for 10 more minutes

Crispy Cornish Hen

Servings: 4
Cooking Time:xx
Ingredients:
- 2 Cornish hens, weighing around 500g each
- 2 tbsp olive oil
- 1 tsp garlic powder
- 1 tsp paprika
- 1.5 tsp Italian seasoning
- 1 tbsp lemon juice
- Salt and pepper to taste

Directions:
1. Preheat your air fryer to 260°C
2. Combine all the ingredients into a bowl (except for the hens) until smooth
3. Brush the hens with the mixture, coating evenly
4. Place in the air fryer basket, with the breast side facing down
5. Cook for 35 minutes
6. Turn over and cook for another 10 minutes
7. Ensure the hens are white in the middle before serving

Chicken And Cheese Chimichangas

Servings: 6
Cooking Time:xx
Ingredients:
- 100g shredded chicken (cooked)
- 150g nacho cheese
- 1 chopped jalapeño pepper
- 6 flour tortillas
- 5 tbsp salsa
- 60g refried beans
- 1 tsp cumin
- 0.5 tsp chill powder
- Salt and pepper to taste

Directions:
1. Take a large mixing bowl and add all of the ingredients, combining well
2. Add ⅓ of the filling to each tortilla and roll into a burrito shape
3. Spray the air fryer with cooking spray and heat to 200°C
4. Place the chimichangas in the air fryer and cook for 7 minutes

Buffalo Chicken Wontons

Servings: 6
Cooking Time:xx
Ingredients:
- 200g shredded chicken
- 1 tbsp buffalo sauce
- 4 tbsp softened cream cheese
- 1 sliced spring onion
- 2 tbsp blue cheese crumbles
- 12 wonton wrappers

Directions:
1. Preheat the air fryer to 200°C
2. Take a bowl and combine the chicken and buffalo sauce

3. In another bowl mix the cream cheese until a smooth consistency has formed and then combine the scallion blue cheese and seasoned chicken
4. Take the wonton wrappers and run wet fingers along each edge
5. Place 1 tbsp of the filling into the centre of the wonton and fold the corners together
6. Cook at 200°C for 3 to 5 minutes, until golden brown

Kale & Rice Chicken Rolls

Servings: 4
Cooking Time: 35 Minutes
Ingredients:
- 4 boneless, skinless chicken thighs
- 2.5ml ground fenugreek seeds
- 200g cooked wild rice
- 2 sundried tomatoes, diced
- 120g chopped kale
- 2 garlic cloves, minced
- 5ml salt
- 1 lemon, juiced
- 120g crumbled feta
- 15ml olive oil

Directions:
1. Preheat the air fryer to 190°C (380°F).
2. Place the chicken thighs between two sheets of plastic wrap. Using a meat mallet or a rolling pin, pound them out to approximately 1/4-inch thickness.
3. In a bowl, combine the cooked wild rice, diced sundried tomatoes, chopped kale, minced garlic, salt, ground fenugreek seeds, and lemon juice. Mix well.
4. Divide the rice mixture equally among the chicken thighs and sprinkle crumbled feta on top.
5. Fold the sides of each chicken thigh over the filling and place them seam-side down in the greased air fryer frying basket.
6. Drizzle the stuffed chicken thighs with olive oil.
7. Roast the stuffed chicken thighs in the air fryer for 12 minutes, then flip them over and continue cooking for an additional 10 minutes or until the chicken is fully cooked and the filling is heated through.
8. Serve your Kale & Rice Chicken Rolls and enjoy!

Coconut Chicken With Apricot-ginger Sauce

Servings: 4
Cooking Time: 8 Minutes Per Batch
Ingredients:
- 680g boneless, skinless chicken tenders, cut in large chunks (about 3cm)
- Salt and pepper
- 125g cornstarch
- 2 eggs
- 15ml milk
- 180g shredded coconut (see below)
- Oil for misting or cooking spray
- Apricot-Ginger Sauce:
- 125ml apricot preserves
- 30ml white vinegar
- 1g ground ginger
- 1g low-sodium soy sauce
- 10g white or yellow onion, grated or finely minced

Directions:
1. Mix all ingredients for the Apricot-Ginger Sauce well and let it sit for flavors to blend while you cook the chicken.
2. Season chicken chunks with salt and pepper to taste.
3. Place cornstarch in a shallow dish.
4. In another shallow dish, beat together eggs and milk.
5. Place coconut in a third shallow dish. (If also using panko breadcrumbs, as suggested below, stir them to mix well.)
6. Spray the air fryer basket with oil or cooking spray.
7. Dip each chicken chunk into cornstarch, shake off excess, and dip in the egg mixture.
8. Shake off excess egg mixture and roll lightly in coconut or coconut mixture. Spray with oil.
9. Place coated chicken chunks in the air fryer basket in a single layer, close together but without sides touching.
10. Cook at 180°C for 4 minutes, stop, and turn chunks over.
11. Cook an additional 4 minutes or until chicken is done inside and coating is crispy brown.
12. Repeat steps 9 through 11 to cook remaining chicken chunks.

Indian Chicken Tandoori

Servings: 2
Cooking Time: 35 Minutes
Ingredients:
- 2 chicken breasts, cubed
- 120ml Greek yogurt (hung curd)
- 1 tsp turmeric powder
- 1 tsp red chili powder
- 1 tsp chaat masala powder
- Pinch of salt

Directions:
1. Preheat the air fryer to 180°C (350°F).

2. In a mixing bowl, combine the Greek yogurt (hung curd), turmeric powder, red chili powder, chaat masala powder, and a pinch of salt. Stir the mixture until it is smooth and free of lumps.
3. Coat the chicken cubes with the yogurt mixture, ensuring they are well-marinated.
4. Cover the bowl and refrigerate for 30 minutes to allow the chicken to marinate.
5. After marinating, place the chicken chunks in a baking pan and drizzle them with the remaining marinade.
6. Bake in the air fryer for 25 minutes or until the chicken is juicy and infused with spices.
7. Serve your Indian Chicken Tandoori while it's still warm.

Italian Herb Stuffed Chicken

Servings: 4
Cooking Time: 30 Minutes
Ingredients:
- 2 tbsp olive oil
- 3 tbsp balsamic vinegar
- 3 garlic cloves, minced
- 1 tomato, diced
- 2 tbsp Italian seasoning
- 1 tbsp chopped fresh basil
- 1 tsp thyme, chopped
- 4 chicken breasts

Directions:
1. Preheat the air fryer to 190°C (370°F).
2. In a medium bowl, combine the olive oil, balsamic vinegar, minced garlic, chopped thyme, diced tomato, half of the Italian seasoning, and basil. Set aside.
3. Cut 4-5 slits into each chicken breast, about ¾ of the way through.
4. Season the chicken breasts with the remaining Italian seasoning.
5. Place the chicken breasts in the greased air fryer frying basket with the slits facing up.
6. Air fry for 7 minutes.
7. Spoon the prepared bruschetta mixture into the slits of the chicken.
8. Continue to air fry for another 3 minutes, ensuring the chicken is thoroughly cooked.
9. Allow the stuffed chicken to rest and cool for a few minutes.
10. Serve and enjoy your Italian Herb Stuffed Chicken!

Chicken Flatbread Pizza With Spinach

Servings: 1
Cooking Time: 15 Minutes
Ingredients:
- 65g cooked chicken breast, cubed
- 30g grated mozzarella
- 1 whole-wheat pita
- 15ml olive oil
- 1 garlic clove, minced
- 0.25 tsp red pepper flakes
- 65g kale
- 15g sliced red onion

Directions:
1. Preheat the air fryer to 190°C (380°F).
2. Lightly brush the top of the pita with olive oil and top with the minced garlic, red pepper flakes, kale, red onion slices, cubed chicken, and mozzarella.
3. Place the pizza into the air fryer basket and cook for 7 minutes or until the cheese is melted and the edges are crispy.
4. Serve and enjoy your Chicken Flatbread Pizza with Spinach!

Gruyère Asparagus & Chicken Quiche

Servings: 4
Cooking Time: 30 Minutes
Ingredients:
- 1 grilled chicken breast, diced
- 60g shredded Gruyère cheese
- 1 premade pie crust
- 2 eggs, beaten
- 60ml milk
- Salt and pepper to taste
- 225g asparagus, sliced
- 1 lemon, zested

Directions:
1. Preheat the air fryer to 180°C (360°F).
2. Carefully press the pie crust into a baking dish, trimming the edges. Prick the dough with a fork a few times.
3. In a mixing bowl, combine the beaten eggs, milk, sliced asparagus, salt, pepper, diced chicken, lemon zest, and half of the Gruyère cheese. Stir until the mixture is well blended.
4. Pour the mixture into the pie crust.
5. Bake in the air fryer for 15 minutes.

6. Sprinkle the remaining Gruyère cheese on top of the quiche filling.
7. Continue to bake for an additional 5 minutes until the quiche is golden brown.
8. Remove from the air fryer and allow it to cool for a few minutes before cutting.
9. Serve sliced and enjoy your Gruyère Asparagus & Chicken Quiche!

Chicken Fried Rice

Servings: 4
Cooking Time:xx
Ingredients:
- 400g cooked white rice
- 400g cooked chicken, diced
- 200g frozen peas and carrots
- 6 tbsp soy sauce
- 1 tbsp vegetable oil
- 1 diced onion

Directions:
1. Take a large bowl and add the rice, vegetable oil and soy sauce and combine well
2. Add the frozen peas, carrots, diced onion and the chicken and mix together well
3. Pour the mixture into a nonstick pan
4. Place the pan into the air fryer
5. Cook at 182C for 20 minutes

Honey Lemon Thyme Glazed Cornish Hen

Servings: 2
Cooking Time: 20 Minutes
Ingredients:
- 1 (900g) Cornish game hen, split in half
- Olive oil
- Salt and freshly ground black pepper
- 1/4 teaspoon dried thyme
- 60ml honey
- 1 tablespoon lemon zest
- Juice of 1 lemon
- 1 1/2 teaspoons chopped fresh thyme leaves
- 1/2 teaspoon soy sauce
- Freshly ground black pepper

Directions:
1. Split the Cornish game hen in half by cutting down each side of the backbone and then cutting through the breast.
2. Brush or lightly spray both halves of the game hen with olive oil and season with salt, pepper, and dried thyme.
3. Preheat the air fryer to 200°C (390°F).
4. Place the game hen halves, skin side down, into the air fryer and air-fry for 5 minutes.
5. Turn the hen halves over and air-fry for an additional 10 minutes.
6. While the hen is cooking, in a small bowl, combine the honey, lemon zest, lemon juice, fresh thyme, soy sauce, and black pepper to create the glaze.
7. When the air fryer timer goes off, brush the honey glaze onto the game hen and continue to air-fry for another 3 to 5 minutes, until the hen is nicely glazed, browned, and reaches an internal temperature of 74°C (165°F).
8. Allow the Cornish hen to rest for 5 minutes before serving. Enjoy your Honey Lemon Thyme Glazed Cornish Hen!

Cajun Chicken Livers

Servings: 2
Cooking Time: 45 Minutes
Ingredients:
- 450 grams chicken livers, rinsed, connective tissue discarded
- 240ml whole milk
- 120 grams cornmeal
- 90 grams flour
- 5 grams salt and black pepper
- 5 grams Cajun seasoning
- 2 eggs
- 180 grams bread crumbs
- 15ml olive oil
- 30ml chopped parsley

Directions:
1. Pat the chicken livers dry with paper towels, then transfer them to a small bowl and pour in the milk and black pepper. Let them sit covered in the fridge for 2 hours.
2. Preheat your air fryer to 190°C (375°F).
3. In a bowl, combine the cornmeal, flour, salt, and Cajun seasoning.
4. In another bowl, beat the eggs.
5. In a third bowl, place the bread crumbs.
6. Dip each chicken liver first into the cornmeal mixture, then into the beaten eggs, and finally into the bread crumbs, ensuring they are well coated.
7. Place the breaded chicken livers in the greased frying basket of the air fryer. Lightly brush the tops with olive oil.
8. Air fry the chicken livers for 16 minutes, turning them once during cooking.
9. Serve your Cajun Chicken Livers right away, sprinkled with chopped parsley.

Family Chicken Fingers

Servings: 4
Cooking Time: 30 Minutes
Ingredients:
- 450g chicken breast fingers
- 1 tbsp chicken seasoning
- ½ tsp mustard powder
- Salt and pepper to taste
- 2 eggs
- 100g bread crumbs

Directions:
1. Preheat the air fryer to 200°C.
2. In a large bowl, combine the chicken fingers with chicken seasoning, mustard powder, salt, and pepper; mix well.
3. Set up two small bowls. In one bowl, beat the eggs. In the second bowl, place the bread crumbs.
4. Dip each chicken finger in the beaten eggs, allowing any excess to drip off, then coat it with the bread crumbs.
5. Place the coated chicken fingers in the air fryer basket. Lightly spray them with cooking oil.
6. Air Fry for 8 minutes, shaking the basket once to ensure even cooking, until the chicken fingers are crispy and cooked through.
7. Serve them warm and enjoy your Family Chicken Fingers!

Asian-style Orange Chicken

Servings: 4
Cooking Time: 25 Minutes
Ingredients:
- 450 grams chicken breasts, cubed
- Salt and pepper to taste
- 6 tablespoons cornstarch
- 240ml orange juice
- 60ml orange marmalade
- 60ml ketchup
- ½ teaspoon ground ginger
- 2 tablespoons soy sauce
- 320 grams edamame beans

Directions:
1. Preheat your air fryer to 190°C (375°F).
2. Season the chicken cubes with salt and pepper to your taste.
3. Coat the chicken with 4 tablespoons of cornstarch and place it on a wire rack. Set aside.
4. In a cake pan, mix the orange juice, marmalade, ketchup, ground ginger, soy sauce, and the remaining cornstarch. Stir in the edamame beans.
5. Place the pan with the sauce and beans in the frying basket of the air fryer.
6. Bake for 5-8 minutes, stirring once during cooking, until the sauce becomes thick and starts bubbling. Remove the pan from the fryer and set it aside.
7. Place the coated chicken cubes in the frying basket and fry for 10-12 minutes, shaking the basket once during cooking.
8. Stir the fried chicken into the sauce and beans in the pan.
9. Return the pan to the fryer and reheat for 2 minutes.
10. Serve your Asian-Style Orange Chicken immediately and enjoy!

Daadi Chicken Salad

Servings: 2
Cooking Time: 30 Minutes
Ingredients:
- 60g chopped golden raisins
- 1 Granny Smith apple, grated
- 2 chicken breasts
- Salt and pepper to taste
- 180ml mayonnaise
- 15ml lime juice
- 5g curry powder
- ½ sliced avocado
- 1 scallion, minced
- 30g chopped pecans
- 5g poppy seeds

Directions:
1. Preheat the air fryer to 180°C.
2. Sprinkle chicken breasts with salt and pepper, place them in the greased frying basket, and Air Fry for 8-10 minutes, tossing once. Let rest for 5 minutes before cutting.
3. In a salad bowl, combine chopped chicken, mayonnaise, lime juice, curry powder, raisins, apple, avocado, scallion, and pecans. Let sit covered in the fridge until ready to eat.
4. Before serving, sprinkle with the poppy seeds.

Satay Chicken Skewers

Servings: 4
Cooking Time:xx
Ingredients:
- 3 chicken breasts, chopped into 3 x 3-cm/1¼ x 1¼-in. cubes
- MARINADE
- 200 ml/¾ cup canned coconut milk (including the thick part from the can)
- 1 plump garlic clove, finely chopped
- 2 teaspoons freshly grated ginger
- 2 tablespoons soy sauce
- 1 heaped tablespoon peanut butter
- 1 tablespoon maple syrup
- 1 tablespoon mild curry powder
- 1 tablespoon fish sauce

Directions:
1. Mix the marinade ingredients thoroughly in a bowl, then toss in the chopped chicken and stir to coat thoroughly. Leave in the fridge to marinate for at least 4 hours.
2. Preheat the air-fryer to 190ºC/375ºF.
3. Thread the chicken onto 8 metal skewers. Add to the preheated air-fryer (you may need to cook these in two batches, depending on the size of your air-fryer). Air-fry for 10 minutes. Check the internal temperature of the chicken has reached at least 74ºC/165ºF using a meat thermometer – if not, cook for another few minutes and then serve.

Classic Chicken Cobb Salad

Servings: 4
Cooking Time: 30 Minutes
Ingredients:
- 115g cooked bacon, crumbled
- 2 chicken breasts, cubed
- 15ml sesame oil
- Salt and pepper to taste
- 4 cups torn romaine lettuce
- 30ml olive oil
- 15ml white wine vinegar
- 2 hard-boiled eggs, sliced
- 2 tomatoes, diced
- 6 radishes, finely sliced
- 30g blue cheese crumbles
- 30g diced red onions
- 1 avocado, diced

Directions:
1. Preheat the air fryer to 180°C (350°F).
2. In a bowl, combine the chicken cubes with sesame oil, salt, and black pepper.
3. Place the seasoned chicken cubes in the air fryer basket and Air Fry for 9 minutes, flipping them once during cooking. Make sure the chicken is thoroughly cooked. Once done, set the chicken aside.
4. In a separate bowl, combine the torn romaine lettuce with olive oil and white wine vinegar. Toss to coat the lettuce.
5. Divide the dressed lettuce between 4 serving bowls.
6. Add the cooked chicken, sliced hard-boiled eggs, crumbled bacon, diced tomatoes, finely sliced radishes, blue cheese crumbles, diced red onions, and diced avocado to each bowl.
7. Serve your Classic Chicken Cobb Salad for a delicious and satisfying meal. Enjoy!

Chicken Tikka Masala

Servings: 4
Cooking Time:xx
Ingredients:
- 100g tikka masala curry pasta
- 200g low fat yogurt
- 600g skinless chicken breasts
- 1 tbsp vegetable oil
- 1 onion, chopped
- 400g can of the whole, peeled tomatoes
- 20ml water
- 1 tbsp sugar
- 2 tbsp lemon juice
- 1 small bunch of chopped coriander leaves

Directions:
1. Take a bowl and combine the tikka masala curry paste with half the yogurt
2. Cut the chicken into strips
3. Preheat the air fryer to 200ºC
4. Add the yogurt mixture and coat the chicken until fully covered
5. Place into the refrigerator for 2 hours
6. Place the oil and onion in the air fryer and cook for 10 minutes
7. Add the marinated chicken, tomatoes, water and the rest of the yogurt and combine
8. Add the sugar and lemon juice and combine again
9. Cook for 15 minutes

Fancy Chicken Piccata

Servings: 4
Cooking Time: 30 Minutes
Ingredients:
- 450g chicken breasts, cut into cutlets
- Salt and pepper to taste
- 2 egg whites
- 150g bread crumbs
- 1 tsp Italian seasoning
- 15g whipped butter
- 120ml chicken broth
- 2g onion powder
- 60ml fino sherry
- Juice of 1 lemon
- 15g capers, drained
- 1 lemon, sliced
- 2 tbsp chopped parsley

Directions:
1. Preheat the air fryer to 190°C.
2. Place the chicken cutlets between two sheets of parchment paper. Pound them to a thickness of about 6mm and season with salt and pepper.
3. In a bowl, beat the egg whites with 5ml of water.
4. In a second bowl, combine the bread crumbs, Italian seasoning, Parmesan cheese, onion powder, and mix well.
5. Dip each chicken cutlet in the egg white mixture and then coat it with the breadcrumb mixture, pressing gently to adhere.
6. Place the coated cutlets in the greased air fryer basket.
7. Air Fry for 6 minutes, flipping the cutlets once during cooking, until they are crispy and golden.
8. While the chicken is cooking, prepare the sauce. In a skillet, melt the butter. Stir in the chicken broth, sherry, lemon juice, lemon slices, and black pepper.
9. Bring the sauce to a boil over high heat and let it simmer until it's reduced by half, which should take about 4 minutes. Remove the skillet from the heat, and remove and discard the lemon slices.
10. Stir in the capers.
11. Plate each chicken cutlet, spoon some sauce over them, and garnish with lemon slices and chopped parsley.

Chicken Flautas

Servings: 6
Cooking Time: 8 Minutes
Ingredients:
- 6 tablespoons whipped cream cheese
- 150g shredded cooked chicken
- 6 tablespoons mild pico de gallo salsa
- 75g shredded Mexican cheese
- 0.5 teaspoon taco seasoning
- Six 20cm flour tortillas
- 100g shredded lettuce
- 50g guacamole

Directions:
1. Preheat the air fryer to 190°C (370°F).
2. In a large bowl, mix the cream cheese, shredded chicken, salsa, shredded cheese, and taco seasoning until well combined.
3. Lay the tortillas on a flat surface. Divide the cheese-and-chicken mixture into 6 equal portions and place the mixture in the center of each tortilla, spreading it evenly, leaving about 2.5cm from the edge of the tortilla.
4. Spray the air fryer basket with olive oil spray. Roll up the flautas and place them edge side down into the basket. Lightly mist the top of the flautas with olive oil spray.
5. Repeat until the air fryer basket is full. You may need to cook these in batches, depending on the size of your air fryer.
6. Cook for 7 minutes, or until the outer edges are browned.
7. Remove from the air fryer basket and serve warm over a bed of shredded lettuce with guacamole on top.

Vegetable Side Dishes Recipes

Roasted Brussels Sprouts With Bacon

Servings: 4
Cooking Time: 20 Minutes
Ingredients:
- 4 slices of thick-cut bacon, chopped (about 115g)
- 450g Brussels sprouts, halved (or quartered if large)
- Freshly ground black pepper

Directions:
1. Preheat the air fryer to 193°C (380°F).
2. Place the chopped bacon in the air fryer basket. Air-fry the bacon for 5 minutes, shaking the basket once or twice during the cooking time.
3. Add the Brussels sprouts to the basket and drizzle a little bacon fat from the bottom of the air fryer drawer into the basket. Toss the Brussels sprouts to coat them with the bacon fat.
4. Air-fry for an additional 15 minutes or until the Brussels sprouts are tender and can be pierced easily with a knife.
5. Season the roasted Brussels sprouts and bacon with freshly ground black pepper.

Za'atar Bell Peppers

Servings: 4
Cooking Time: 40 Minutes
Ingredients:
- 1 red bell pepper
- 1 orange bell pepper
- 1 yellow bell pepper
- 2 tsp Za'atar seasoning
- 1 tbsp lemon zest
- ½ tsp salt

Directions:
1. Preheat your air fryer to 188°C (370°F).
2. Pierce each of the bell peppers a few times with a fork to allow steam to escape during cooking.
3. Place the bell peppers in the greased air fryer basket.
4. Air fry for 12-15 minutes, shaking the basket once during cooking, until the peppers become slightly charred.
5. Remove the bell peppers from the air fryer and place them in a small bowl. Cover the bowl and let the peppers sit for 10 minutes; this will help steam them and make it easier to remove the skins.
6. After 10 minutes, peel the skin off the peppers, remove the seeds, and slice them.
7. Sprinkle the sliced peppers with Za'atar seasoning, lemon zest, and salt.
8. Serve your Za'atar Bell Peppers as a flavorful and colourful side dish.

Cheese-rice Stuffed Bell Peppers

Servings: 4
Cooking Time: 30 Minutes
Ingredients:
- 2 red bell peppers, halved, seeds and stem removed
- 225 grams cooked brown rice
- 2 tomatoes, diced
- 1 garlic clove, minced
- Salt and pepper to taste
- 115 grams goat cheese
- 45 ml basil, chopped
- 45 ml oregano, chopped
- 15 ml parsley, chopped
- 30 grams grated Parmesan

Directions:
1. Preheat your air fryer to 180°C (360°F).
2. In a bowl, combine the cooked brown rice, diced tomatoes, minced garlic, salt, and pepper. Mix well.
3. Divide the rice filling evenly among the bell pepper halves.
4. In a small bowl, combine the goat cheese, chopped basil, chopped parsley, and chopped oregano.
5. Sprinkle each bell pepper with the herbed goat cheese mixture.
6. Arrange the stuffed bell peppers in the air fryer basket.
7. Bake for 20 minutes in the air fryer.
8. Serve your Cheese-Rice Stuffed Bell Peppers topped with grated Parmesan and parsley. Enjoy!

Green Dip With Pine Nuts

Servings: 3
Cooking Time: 30 Minutes
Ingredients:
- 285g canned artichokes, chopped
- 10g grated Parmesan cheese
- 285g spinach, chopped
- 2 scallions, finely chopped
- 65g pine nuts
- 120ml milk
- 45ml lemon juice
- 10g tapioca flour

- 5ml allspice

Directions:
1. Preheat the air fryer to 180°C (360°F).
2. Arrange the chopped spinach, chopped artichokes, and finely chopped scallions in a pan. Set it aside.
3. In a food processor, blend the pine nuts, milk, lemon juice, grated Parmesan cheese, tapioca flour, and allspice on high until the mixture is smooth.
4. Pour the blended mixture over the vegetables in the pan.
5. Bake in the air fryer for 20 minutes, stirring every 5 minutes to ensure even cooking.
6. Serve your Green Dip with Pine Nuts.

Truffle Vegetable Croquettes

Servings: 4
Cooking Time: 40 Minutes

Ingredients:
- 2 cooked potatoes, mashed
- 1 cooked carrot, mashed
- 1 tbsp onion, minced
- 2 eggs, beaten
- 2 tbsp melted butter
- 1 tbsp truffle oil
- ½ tbsp flour
- Salt and pepper to taste

Directions:
1. Preheat your air fryer to 180°C (350°F).
2. In a bowl, sift the flour and season it with salt and pepper. Stir to combine.
3. In a separate bowl, mix together the mashed potatoes, mashed carrot, minced onion, melted butter, and truffle oil until well combined.
4. Shape the potato mixture into small bite-sized patties.
5. Dip each potato patty into the beaten eggs, ensuring they are thoroughly coated.
6. Roll the egg-coated patties in the flour mixture to cover all sides.
7. Grease the frying basket of your air fryer.
8. Arrange the croquettes in the greased frying basket in a single layer.
9. Air fry for 14-16 minutes, shaking the basket halfway through the cooking time, until the croquettes are crispy and golden.
10. Serve hot and enjoy your Truffle Vegetable Croquettes!

Greek-inspired Ratatouille

Servings: 6
Cooking Time: 55 Minutes

Ingredients:
- 150g cherry tomatoes
- 1/2 bulb fennel, finely sliced
- 2 russet potatoes, cubed
- 120g tomatoes, cubed
- 1 eggplant, cubed
- 1 zucchini, cubed
- 1 red onion, chopped
- 1 red bell pepper, chopped
- 2 garlic cloves, minced
- 5ml dried mint
- 5ml dried parsley
- 5ml dried oregano
- Salt and pepper to taste
- 1.25ml red pepper flakes
- 80ml olive oil
- 1 can tomato paste
- 60ml vegetable broth

Directions:
1. Preheat the air fryer to 160°C (320°F).
2. In a large bowl, mix together the potatoes, cherry tomatoes, fennel, eggplant, zucchini, onion, red bell pepper, minced garlic, dried mint, dried parsley, dried oregano, salt, black pepper, and red pepper flakes.
3. In a small bowl, whisk together the olive oil, tomato paste, vegetable broth, and 60ml of water.
4. Toss the vegetable mixture with the prepared olive oil and tomato paste mixture to coat them evenly.
5. Pour the coated vegetables into the air frying basket in a single layer.
6. Roast for 20 minutes, then stir well and spread them out again.
7. Roast for an additional 10 minutes, stir again, and then cook for another 10 minutes or until the vegetables are tender and slightly caramelized.
8. Serve your Greek-Inspired Ratatouille and enjoy!

Almond Green Beans

Servings: 4
Cooking Time: 20 Minutes

Ingredients:
- 200 grams green beans, trimmed
- 30 grams slivered almonds
- 28 grams butter, melted
- Salt and pepper to taste
- 10 ml lemon juice
- Lemon zest and slices

Directions:
1. Preheat the air fryer to 190°C (375°F).

2. Place slivered almonds in the frying basket and Air Fry for 2 minutes, tossing once. Set aside in a small bowl.
3. In a separate bowl, combine the melted butter, salt, pepper, lemon juice, and green beans, tossing to coat.
4. Place the coated green beans in the frying basket and Air Fry for 10 minutes, tossing once during cooking.
5. Transfer the cooked green beans to a large serving dish.
6. Scatter the roasted almonds over the green beans and toss.
7. Serve immediately, garnished with lemon zest and lemon slices. Enjoy!

Veggie Fritters

Servings: 4
Cooking Time: 35 Minutes
Ingredients:
- 25g crumbled feta cheese
- 1 grated courgette (zucchini)
- 25g Parmesan cheese
- 15g minced onion
- 5g garlic powder
- 15g plain flour
- 15g cornmeal
- 15g butter, melted
- 1 egg
- 10g chopped dill
- 10g chopped parsley
- Salt and pepper to taste
- 60g breadcrumbs

Directions:
1. Preheat your air fryer to 180°C (350°F).
2. Squeeze the grated courgette (zucchini) between paper towels to remove excess moisture.
3. In a bowl, combine all the ingredients except for the breadcrumbs. Mix until well combined.
4. Form the mixture into 12 balls, each about 2 tablespoons in size.
5. Place the breadcrumbs in a shallow bowl.
6. Roll each fritter ball in the breadcrumbs, ensuring they are coated on all sides.
7. Arrange the fritters on an ungreased pizza pan or tray.
8. Place the pizza pan or tray in the air fryer frying basket.
9. Air fry the fritters for 11 minutes, flipping them once during cooking for even browning.
10. Once the fritters are golden brown and cooked through, remove them from the air fryer.
11. Serve your delicious Veggie Fritters.

Spiced Pumpkin Wedges

Servings: 4
Cooking Time: 35 Minutes
Ingredients:
- 600g pumpkin, cubed
- 2 tablespoons olive oil
- Salt and pepper to taste
- 1/4 teaspoon pumpkin pie spice
- 1 tablespoon fresh thyme leaves
- 25g grated Parmesan cheese

Directions:
1. Preheat your air fryer to 180°C (360°F).
2. In a large bowl, combine the cubed pumpkin with olive oil, salt, pumpkin pie spice, freshly ground black pepper, and fresh thyme leaves. Stir until the pumpkin is evenly coated.
3. Place this pumpkin mixture into the air fryer basket.
4. Roast the pumpkin in the air fryer for 18-20 minutes, stirring once during cooking, until the pumpkin is tender and slightly crispy.
5. Sprinkle the roasted pumpkin wedges with grated Parmesan cheese.
6. Serve your Spiced Pumpkin Wedges and enjoy!

Goat Cheese Stuffed Portobellos

Servings: 4
Cooking Time: 35 Minutes
Ingredients:
- 240ml baby spinach
- 180g crumbled goat cheese
- 10g grated Parmesan cheese
- 4 portobello caps, cleaned
- Salt and pepper to taste
- 2 tomatoes, chopped
- 1 leek, chopped
- 1 garlic clove, minced
- 60ml chopped parsley
- 30ml panko bread crumbs
- 15ml chopped oregano
- 15ml olive oil
- Balsamic glaze for drizzling

Directions:
1. Brush the portobello mushroom caps with olive oil and sprinkle with salt.
2. In a bowl, mix together the baby spinach, crumbled goat cheese, grated Parmesan cheese, chopped tomatoes, chopped leek, minced garlic, chopped parsley, panko bread crumbs,

chopped oregano, and olive oil. Season with salt and pepper to taste.
3. Fill each mushroom cap with the mixture.
4. Preheat the air fryer to 190°C (370°F).
5. Place the stuffed mushroom caps in the greased air fryer basket.
6. Air fry for 10-12 minutes or until the tops are golden, and the mushrooms are tender.
7. Carefully transfer the stuffed mushrooms to a serving dish.
8. Drizzle with balsamic glaze.
9. Serve warm and enjoy your Goat Cheese Stuffed Portobellos!

Glazed Carrots

Servings: 4
Cooking Time: 10 Minutes
Ingredients:
- 10ml honey
- 5ml orange juice
- 2.5ml grated orange rind
- A pinch of ginger
- 450g baby carrots
- 10ml olive oil
- A pinch of salt

Directions:
1. In a small bowl, combine the honey, orange juice, grated orange rind, and a pinch of ginger. Set aside.
2. Toss the baby carrots with olive oil and a pinch of salt to coat them well, then place them in the air fryer basket.
3. Cook at 200°C (390°F) for 5 minutes.
4. After 5 minutes, shake the basket to stir the carrots a little, and continue cooking for an additional 4 minutes, or until the carrots are barely tender.
5. Transfer the cooked carrots to an air fryer baking pan.
6. Stir the honey mixture to combine it well, then pour the glaze over the carrots and stir to coat them evenly.
7. Cook at 180°C (360°F) for 1 minute, or just until the carrots are heated through and the glaze is well incorporated.

Fried Corn On The Cob

Servings: 2
Cooking Time: 10 Minutes
Ingredients:
- 22.5 ml Regular or low-fat mayonnaise (not fat-free; gluten-free, if a concern)
- 7.5 ml Minced garlic
- 1.25 ml Table salt
- 180 ml Plain panko bread crumbs (gluten-free, if a concern)
- 3 10 cm lengths husked and de-silked corn on the cob
- Vegetable oil spray

Directions:
1. Preheat your air fryer to 200°C (400°F).
2. Stir the mayonnaise, garlic, and salt in a small bowl until well combined. Spread the panko on a dinner plate.
3. Brush the mayonnaise mixture over the kernels of a piece of corn on the cob. Set the corn in the bread crumbs, then roll, pressing gently, to coat it. Lightly coat it with vegetable oil spray. Set it aside, then coat the remaining piece(s) of corn in the same way.
4. Set the coated corn on the cob in the basket with as much air space between the pieces as possible. Air-fry undisturbed for 10 minutes, or until they are brown and crisp along the coating.
5. Use kitchen tongs to gently transfer the pieces of corn to a wire rack. Cool for 5 minutes before serving your Fried Corn on the Cob. Enjoy!

Stuffed Avocados

Servings: 4
Cooking Time: 8 Minutes
Ingredients:
- 150g frozen shoepeg corn, thawed
- 200g cooked black beans
- 30g diced onion
- 1.25ml cumin
- 10ml lime juice, plus extra for serving
- Salt and pepper
- 2 large avocados, split in half, pit removed

Directions:
1. Mix together the corn, black beans, diced onion, cumin, and lime juice. Season to taste with salt and pepper.
2. Scoop out some of the flesh from the center of each avocado and set it aside.
3. Divide the corn mixture evenly between the avocado cavities.
4. Set the avocado halves in the air fryer basket and cook at 180°C (360°F) for 8 minutes, or until the corn mixture is hot.
5. Season the avocado flesh that you scooped out with a squirt of lime juice, salt, and pepper. Spoon it over the cooked halves.
6. Serve immediately.

Succulent Roasted Peppers

Servings: 2
Cooking Time: 35 Minutes
Ingredients:
- 2 red bell peppers
- 2 tablespoons olive oil
- Salt to taste
- 1 teaspoon dill, chopped

Directions:
1. Preheat the air fryer to 200°C.
2. Remove the tops and bottoms of the peppers. Cut along the rib sections and discard the seeds.
3. Combine the bell peppers and olive oil in a bowl, ensuring they are well coated.
4. Place bell peppers in the frying basket and roast for 24 minutes, flipping once during cooking.
5. Transfer the roasted peppers to a small bowl and cover for 15 minutes. Then, peel and discard the skins.
6. Sprinkle with salt and chopped dill, and serve.

Yellow Squash

Servings: 4
Cooking Time: 10 Minutes
Ingredients:
- 1 large yellow squash (about 1½ cups)
- 2 eggs
- 60ml buttermilk
- 75g panko breadcrumbs
- 30g white cornmeal
- ½ teaspoon salt
- Oil for misting or cooking spray

Directions:
1. Preheat your air fryer to 199°C (390°F).
2. Cut the yellow squash into 6mm (¼ inch) slices.
3. In a shallow dish, beat together the eggs and buttermilk.
4. In a sealable plastic bag or a container with a lid, combine 30g (¼ cup) panko crumbs, white cornmeal, and salt. Shake well to mix.
5. Place the remaining 45g (¾ cup) panko crumbs in a separate shallow dish.
6. Dip all the squash slices into the egg/buttermilk mixture, stirring to coat.
7. Remove the squash from the egg/buttermilk mixture with a slotted spoon, letting excess liquid drip off, and transfer them to the panko/cornmeal mixture. Close the bag or container and shake well to coat.
8. Remove the squash slices from the crumb mixture, letting any excess fall off. Return the squash to the egg/buttermilk mixture, stirring gently to coat. If needed, add a little more buttermilk to ensure all the squash is coated.
9. Remove each squash slice from the egg wash and dip it into a dish containing the remaining 45g (¾ cup) panko crumbs.
10. Mist the squash slices with oil or use cooking spray and place them in the air fryer basket. The squash should be in a single layer, but it's okay if they crowd together and overlap slightly.
11. Cook at 199°C (390°F) for 5 minutes. Shake the basket to break up any that have stuck together. Mist them again with oil or cooking spray.
12. Cook for an additional 5 minutes and check for doneness. If necessary, mist them again with oil and cook for an additional two minutes or until the squash slices are golden brown and crisp.

Buttery Radish Wedges

Servings: 2
Cooking Time: 20 Minutes
Ingredients:
- 30 grams butter, melted
- 2 cloves garlic, minced
- 1.25 ml salt
- 20 radishes, quartered
- 30 grams feta cheese crumbles
- 15 ml chopped parsley

Directions:
1. Preheat your air fryer to 190°C (370°F).
2. In a bowl, combine the melted butter, minced garlic, and salt.
3. Add the quartered radishes to the bowl and toss them in the butter mixture until well coated.
4. Place the radish wedges in the air fryer basket.
5. Roast for 10 minutes, shaking the basket once during cooking.
6. Transfer the roasted radishes to a large serving dish.
7. Stir in the feta cheese crumbles and scatter with chopped parsley.
8. Serve your Buttery Radish Wedges right away. Enjoy!

Toasted Choco-nuts

Servings: 2
Cooking Time: 10 Minutes
Ingredients:
- 200g almonds
- 10ml maple syrup
- 30g cacao powder

Directions:

1. Preheat the air fryer to 180°C (350°F).
2. Spread the almonds in a single layer in the air fryer frying basket.
3. Bake the almonds for 3 minutes, then shake the basket for even cooking.
4. Continue to bake for another 1 minute or until the almonds are golden brown.
5. Remove the toasted almonds from the air fryer and transfer them to a bowl.
6. Drizzle the almonds with maple syrup and toss them to coat evenly.
7. Sprinkle the cacao powder over the almonds and toss until they are well coated with the cacao powder.
8. Allow the toasted choco-nuts to cool completely.
9. Store the toasted choco-nuts in an airtight container at room temperature for up to 2 weeks or in the fridge for up to a month.

Fried Green Tomatoes With Sriracha Mayo

Servings: 4
Cooking Time: 12 Minutes
Ingredients:
- 3 green tomatoes
- salt and freshly ground black pepper
- 75 grams all-purpose flour*
- 2 eggs
- 120 ml buttermilk
- 75 grams panko breadcrumbs*
- 75 grams cornmeal
- olive oil, in a spray bottle
- fresh thyme sprigs or chopped fresh chives
- Sriracha Mayo
- 120 ml mayonnaise
- 1 to 2 tablespoons sriracha hot sauce
- 15 ml milk

Directions:
1. Cut the tomatoes into 6 mm (¼-inch) slices. Pat them dry with a clean kitchen towel and season generously with salt and pepper.
2. Set up a dredging station using three shallow dishes. Place the flour in the first shallow dish, whisk the eggs and buttermilk together in the second dish, and combine the panko breadcrumbs and cornmeal in the third dish.
3. Preheat the air fryer to 200°C (400°F).
4. Dredge the tomato slices in flour to coat on all sides. Then dip them into the egg mixture and finally press them into the breadcrumbs to coat all sides of the tomato.
5. Spray or brush the air fryer basket with olive oil. Transfer 3 to 4 tomato slices into the basket and spray the top with olive oil. Air-fry the tomatoes at 200°C (400°F) for 8 minutes. Flip them over, spray the other side with oil and air-fry for an additional 4 minutes until golden brown.
6. While the tomatoes are cooking, make the sriracha mayo. Combine the mayonnaise, 1 to 2 tablespoons of sriracha hot sauce, and milk in a small bowl. Stir well until the mixture is smooth. Add more sriracha sauce to taste.
7. When the tomatoes are done, transfer them to a cooling rack or a platter lined with paper towels so the bottom does not get soggy. Before serving, carefully stack all the tomatoes into the air fryer and air-fry at 180°C (350°F) for 1 to 2 minutes to heat them back up.
8. Serve the fried green tomatoes hot with the sriracha mayo on the side. Season one last time with salt and freshly ground black pepper and garnish with sprigs of fresh thyme or chopped fresh chives. Enjoy!

Stunning Apples & Onions

Servings: 4
Cooking Time: 30 Minutes
Ingredients:
- 2 peeled McIntosh apples, sliced
- 1 shallot, sliced
- 2 teaspoons canola oil
- 2 tablespoons brown sugar
- 1 tablespoon honey
- 1 tablespoon butter, melted
- ½ teaspoon sea salt

Directions:
1. Preheat the air fryer to 160°C.
2. Toss the shallot slices with oil in a bowl until coated. Put the bowl in the fryer and bake for 5 minutes.
3. Remove the bowl and add the apples, brown sugar, honey, melted butter, and sea salt. Stir well to combine.
4. Put the bowl back into the fryer and bake for 10-12 more minutes or until the onions and apples are tender.
5. Stir again and serve.

Mexican-style Roasted Corn

Servings: 3
Cooking Time: 14 Minutes
Ingredients:
- 45g butter, melted and cooled
- 10ml minced garlic
- 3.75ml ground cumin
- Up to 3.75ml red pepper flakes
- 1.25ml table salt

- 3 cold 10cm lengths husked and de-silked corn on the cob
- Minced fresh cilantro leaves
- Crumbled queso fresco

Directions:
1. Preheat the air fryer to 200°C (400°F).
2. Mix the melted butter, minced garlic, ground cumin, red pepper flakes (use as much as you prefer for spiciness), and salt in a large zip-closed plastic bag.
3. Add the cold corn pieces to the bag, seal it, and massage the butter mixture into the surface of the corn.
4. When the air fryer is at temperature, take the corn pieces out of the plastic bag and place them in the basket with as much air space between the pieces as possible.
5. Air-fry undisturbed for 14 minutes, or until the corn is golden brown and possibly charred in a few small spots.
6. Use kitchen tongs to gently transfer the corn pieces to a serving platter.
7. Sprinkle each piece with minced fresh cilantro and crumbled queso fresco.
8. Serve warm.

Mashed Potato Tots

Servings: 18
Cooking Time: 10 Minutes

Ingredients:
- 1 medium potato or 240ml cooked mashed potatoes
- 15ml real bacon bits
- 30ml chopped green onions, tops only
- 1.25ml onion powder
- 5ml dried chopped chives
- Salt
- 30ml flour
- 1 egg white, beaten
- 120ml panko breadcrumbs
- Oil for misting or cooking spray

Directions:
1. If using cooked mashed potatoes, skip to step 4.
2. Peel the potato and cut it into 1.25cm (½-inch) cubes (smaller pieces cook more quickly). Place them in a saucepan, add water to cover, and heat to a boil. Lower the heat slightly and continue cooking just until tender, about 10 minutes.
3. Drain the potatoes and place them in ice-cold water. Allow them to cool for a minute or two, then drain well and mash.
4. Preheat the air fryer to 200°C (390°F).
5. In a large bowl, mix together the mashed potatoes, bacon bits, chopped green onions, onion powder, chives, and salt to taste. Add the flour and stir well.
6. Place the panko breadcrumbs on a sheet of wax paper.
7. For each tot, use about 2 teaspoons of potato mixture. To shape, drop the measured potato mixture onto the panko crumbs and push the crumbs up and around the potatoes to coat the edges. Then turn the tot over to coat the other side with crumbs.
8. Mist the tots with oil or cooking spray and place them in the air fryer basket, ensuring they are crowded but not stacked.
9. Cook at 200°C (390°F) for 10 minutes, or until they are browned and crispy.
10. Repeat steps 8 and 9 to cook the remaining tots.

Fried Pearl Onions With Balsamic Vinegar And Basil

Servings: 2
Cooking Time: 10 Minutes

Ingredients:
- 1 pound fresh pearl onions
- 1 tablespoon olive oil
- Salt and freshly ground black pepper
- 1 teaspoon high-quality aged balsamic vinegar
- 1 tablespoon chopped fresh basil leaves (or mint)

Directions:
1. Preheat the air fryer to 400°F (200°C).
2. Decide whether you want to peel the onions before or after they cook. Peeling them ahead of time is a little more laborious. Peeling after they cook is easier but messier since the onions are hot. If you peel them first, trim the tiny root of the onions off and remove any loose papery skins. Toss the pearl onions with olive oil, salt, and freshly ground black pepper.
3. Air-fry the pearl onions for 10 minutes, shaking the basket a couple of times during the cooking process. If your pearl onions are very large, you may need to add a couple of minutes to this cooking time.
4. Let the onions cool slightly, then slip off any remaining skins.
5. Toss the onions with balsamic vinegar and chopped basil (or mint).
6. Serve and enjoy your Fried Pearl Onions with Balsamic Vinegar and Basil!

Bacon-wrapped Asparagus

Servings: 4
Cooking Time: 10 Minutes
Ingredients:
- 1 tablespoon extra-virgin olive oil
- 1/2 teaspoon sea salt
- 1/4 cup grated Parmesan cheese
- 450 grams asparagus, ends trimmed
- 8 slices bacon

Directions:
1. Preheat the air fryer to 190°C (380°F).
2. In a large bowl, mix together the extra-virgin olive oil, sea salt, and grated Parmesan cheese. Toss the asparagus in the olive oil mixture to coat them.
3. Divide the asparagus into 8 bundles. Wrap 1 slice of bacon around each bundle, ensuring the bacon is spread evenly across the bundle without overlapping.
4. Place the asparagus bundles into the air fryer basket, making sure they are not touching. You may need to work in batches.
5. Cook for 8 minutes, then check for doneness. If needed, cook for an additional 2 minutes until the bacon is crispy and the asparagus is tender.

Fried Cauliflower With Parmesan Lemon Dressing

Servings: 2
Cooking Time: 12 Minutes
Ingredients:
- 450 grams cauliflower florets (about half a large head)
- 15 ml olive oil
- Salt and freshly ground black pepper
- 5 ml finely chopped lemon zest
- 15 ml fresh lemon juice (about half a lemon)
- 30 grams grated Parmigiano-Reggiano cheese
- 60 ml extra virgin olive oil
- 1.25 ml salt
- Lots of freshly ground black pepper
- 15 ml chopped fresh parsley

Directions:
1. Preheat your air fryer to 200°C (400°F).
2. Toss the cauliflower florets with the olive oil, salt, and freshly ground black pepper. Air-fry for 12 minutes, shaking the basket a couple of times during the cooking process.
3. While the cauliflower is frying, make the dressing. Combine the lemon zest, lemon juice, Parmigiano-Reggiano cheese, and olive oil in a small bowl. Season with salt and lots of freshly ground black pepper. Stir in the parsley.
4. Turn the fried cauliflower out onto a serving platter and drizzle the dressing over the top. Enjoy your Fried Cauliflower with Parmesan Lemon Dressing!

Fried Eggplant Balls

Servings: 4
Cooking Time: 40 Minutes
Ingredients:
- 1 medium eggplant (about 450 grams)
- Olive oil
- Salt and freshly ground black pepper
- 100 grams grated Parmesan cheese
- 200 grams fresh breadcrumbs
- 30 ml chopped fresh parsley
- 30 ml chopped fresh basil
- 1 clove garlic, minced
- 1 egg, lightly beaten
- 50 grams fine dried breadcrumbs

Directions:
1. Preheat your air fryer to 200°C (400°F).
2. Quarter the eggplant by cutting it in half both lengthwise and horizontally. Make a few slashes in the flesh of the eggplant but not through the skin. Brush the cut surface of the eggplant generously with olive oil and transfer to the air fryer basket, cut side up. Air-fry for 10 minutes. Turn the eggplant quarters cut side down and air-fry for another 15 minutes or until the eggplant is soft all the way through. You may need to rotate the pieces in the air fryer so that they cook evenly. Transfer the eggplant to a cutting board to cool.
3. Place the Parmesan cheese, the fresh breadcrumbs, fresh herbs, garlic, and egg in a food processor. Scoop the flesh out of the eggplant, discarding the skin and any pieces that are tough. You should have about 225-300 grams of eggplant. Add the eggplant to the food processor and process everything together until smooth. Season with salt and pepper. Refrigerate the mixture for at least 30 minutes.
4. Place the dried breadcrumbs into a shallow dish or onto a plate. Scoop heaping tablespoons of the eggplant mixture into the dried breadcrumbs. Roll the dollops of eggplant in the breadcrumbs and then shape them into small balls. You should have 16 to 18 eggplant balls at the end. Refrigerate until you are ready to air-fry.
5. Preheat the air fryer to 175°C (350°F).
6. Spray the eggplant balls and the air fryer basket with olive oil. Air-fry the eggplant balls for 15 minutes, rotating them during the cooking process to brown evenly. Enjoy your Fried Eggplant Balls!

Baked Shishito Peppers

Servings: 2
Cooking Time: 15 Minutes
Ingredients:
- 170 grams shishito peppers
- 5 ml olive oil
- 5 ml salt
- 60 ml soy sauce

Directions:
1. Preheat your air fryer to 190°C (375°F).
2. In a mixing bowl, combine all the ingredients.
3. Place the shishito peppers in the air fryer basket.
4. Bake for 8 minutes, or until the peppers are blistered, shaking the basket once during cooking.
5. Serve the baked shishito peppers with soy sauce for dipping. Enjoy!

Spiced Roasted Acorn Squash

Servings: 2
Cooking Time: 45 Minutes
Ingredients:
- 1/2 acorn squash
- 5 ml melted butter
- 10 ml light brown sugar
- 0.125 ml ground cinnamon
- 30 ml hot sauce
- 60 ml maple syrup

Directions:
1. Preheat the air fryer to 200°C (392°F).
2. Slice off about 0.6 cm from the side of the squash half to make it sit flat like a bowl.
3. In a bowl, combine the melted butter, light brown sugar, ground cinnamon, hot sauce, and maple syrup. Mix well.
4. Brush the mixture over the top of the squash, making sure to coat it evenly. Pour any remaining mixture into the middle of the squash.
5. Place the squash in the frying basket of the air fryer.
6. Roast at 200°C (392°F) for 35 minutes or until the squash is tender and can be easily pierced with a fork.
7. Remove the squash from the air fryer and let it cool slightly.
8. Cut it in half and divide it between 2 serving plates.
9. Serve and enjoy your Spiced Roasted Acorn Squash!

Tofu & Broccoli Salad

Servings: 4
Cooking Time: 17 Minutes
Ingredients:
- Broccoli Salad
- 400g fresh broccoli, cut into bite-size pieces
- 120g red onion, chopped
- 50g raisins or dried cherries
- 90g sliced almonds
- 120ml Asian-style salad dressing
- Tofu
- 115g extra firm tofu
- 1 teaspoon smoked paprika
- 1 teaspoon onion powder
- 1/4 teaspoon salt
- 20g cornstarch
- 15ml extra virgin olive oil

Directions:
1. Place several folded paper towels on a plate and set tofu on top. Cover tofu with another folded paper towel, put another plate on top, and add heavy items such as canned goods to weigh it down. Press tofu for 30 minutes.
2. While tofu is draining, combine all salad ingredients in a large bowl. Toss together well, cover, and chill until ready to serve.
3. Cut the tofu into small cubes, about 1cm thick. Sprinkle the cubes on top and bottom with the paprika, onion powder, and salt.
4. Place cornstarch in a small plastic bag, add tofu, and shake until cubes are well coated.
5. Place olive oil in another small plastic bag, add coated tofu, and shake to coat well.
6. Preheat the air fryer to 165°C (330°F).
7. Cook the coated tofu cubes in the air fryer for 17 minutes or until they are as crispy as you like.
8. To serve, stir the chilled salad well, divide it among 4 plates, and top with the fried tofu.

Hot Okra Wedges

Servings: 2
Cooking Time: 35 Minutes
Ingredients:
- 240g okra, sliced
- 100g breadcrumbs
- 2 eggs, beaten
- A pinch of black pepper
- 5ml crushed red peppers
- 10ml hot Tabasco sauce

Directions:
1. Preheat the air fryer to 175°C (350°F).
2. Place the beaten eggs and Tabasco sauce in a bowl and stir thoroughly; set aside.
3. In a separate mixing bowl, combine the breadcrumbs, crushed red peppers, and black pepper.

4. Dip the okra slices into the beaten eggs and Tabasco sauce mixture, then coat them in the breadcrumb mixture.
5. Lay the coated okra pieces on the greased air fryer basket.
6. Air fry for 14-16 minutes, shaking the basket several times during cooking.
7. When ready, the okra will be crispy and golden brown.
8. Serve your Hot Okra Wedges.

Italian Breaded Eggplant Rounds

Servings: 4
Cooking Time: 30 Minutes
Ingredients:
- 1 eggplant, sliced into rounds
- 1 egg
- 120ml bread crumbs
- 5ml onion powder
- 2.5ml Italian seasoning
- 2.5ml garlic salt
- 2.5ml paprika
- 15ml olive oil

Directions:
1. Preheat the air fryer to 180°C (360°F).
2. Whisk the egg and 15ml of water in a bowl until frothy.
3. In a separate bowl, mix the bread crumbs, onion powder, Italian seasoning, garlic salt, and paprika.
4. Dip the eggplant slices into the egg mixture, then coat them with the bread crumb mixture.
5. Place the coated eggplant slices in a single layer in the air fryer basket.
6. Drizzle the olive oil over the slices.
7. Air fry for 23-25 minutes, turning once, until they are golden and crispy.
8. Serve your Italian Breaded Eggplant Rounds warm.

Charred Radicchio Salad

Servings: 4
Cooking Time: 5 Minutes
Ingredients:
- 2 Small 140 to 170-gram radicchio heads
- 45 ml Olive oil
- 2.5 ml Table salt
- 30 ml Balsamic vinegar
- Up to 1.25 ml Red pepper flakes

Directions:
1. Preheat your air fryer to 190°C (375°F).
2. Cut the radicchio heads into quarters through the stem end.
3. Brush the olive oil over the quarters, making sure to get it between the leaves along the cut sides. Sprinkle the radicchio quarters with the salt.
4. Once the air fryer reaches temperature, place the radicchio quarters cut sides up in the basket with as much airspace between them as possible. They should not touch.
5. Air-fry undisturbed for 5 minutes, but watch them carefully as they can burn quickly. The radicchio should become blackened in spots and soft.
6. Use a nonstick-safe spatula to transfer the quarters to a cutting board. Allow them to cool for a minute or two.
7. Cut out and discard the thick stems inside the heads. Chop the remaining radicchio into bite-size pieces and place them in a bowl.
8. Add the balsamic vinegar and red pepper flakes. Toss well and serve your Charred Radicchio Salad warm. Enjoy!

Desserts Recipes

Lemon Buns

Servings: 12
Cooking Time:xx
Ingredients:
- 100g butter
- 100g caster sugar
- 2 eggs
- 100g self raising flour
- ½ tsp vanilla essence
- 1 tsp cherries
- 50g butter
- 100g icing sugar
- ½ small lemon rind and juice

Directions:
1. Preheat the air fryer to 170°C
2. Cream the 100g butter, sugar and vanilla together until light and fluffy
3. Beat in the eggs one at a time adding a little flour with each
4. Fold in the remaining flour
5. Half fill bun cases with the mix, place in the air fryer and cook for 8 minutes
6. Cream 50g butter then mix in the icing sugar, stir in the lemon
7. Slice the top off each bun and create a butterfly shape using the icing to hold together. Add a 1/3 cherry to each one

Apple And Cinnamon Puff Pastry Pies

Servings:8
Cooking Time:20 Minutes
Ingredients:
- 4 tbsp butter
- 4 tbsp white sugar
- 2 tbsp brown sugar
- 1 tsp cinnamon
- 1 tsp nutmeg
- 1 tsp salt
- 4 apples, peeled and diced
- 2 large sheets puff pastry
- 1 egg

Directions:
1. Preheat the air fryer to 180 °C / 350 °F. Remove the mesh basket from the machine and line it with parchment paper.
2. In a bowl, whisk together the butter, white sugar, brown sugar, cinnamon, nutmeg, and salt.
3. Place the apples in a heatproof baking dish and coat them in the butter and sugar mixture. Transfer to the air fryer and cook for 10 minutes.
4. Meanwhile, roll out the pastry on a clean, floured surface. Cut the sheets into 8 equal parts.
5. Once the apples are hot and softened, evenly spread the mixture between the pastry sheets. Fold the sheets over to cover the apple and gently press the edges using a fork or your fingers to seal the mixture in.
6. Beat the egg in a bowl and use a brush to coat the top of each pastry sheet.
7. Carefully transfer the filled pastry sheets to the prepared air fryer basket, close the lid, and cook for 10 minutes until the pastry is golden and crispy.

New York Cheesecake

Servings: 8
Cooking Time:xx
Ingredients:
- 225g plain flour
- 100g brown sugar
- 100g butter
- 50g melted butter
- 1 tbsp vanilla essence
- 750g soft cheese
- 2 cups caster sugar
- 3 large eggs
- 50ml quark

Directions:
1. Add the flour, sugar, and 100g butter to a bowl and mix until combined. Form into biscuit shapes place in the air fryer and cook for 15 minutes at 180°C
2. Grease a springform tin
3. Break the biscuits up and mix with the melted butter, press firmly into the tin
4. Mix the soft cheese and sugar in a bowl until creamy, add the eggs and vanilla and mix. Mix in the quark
5. Pour the cheesecake batter into the pan
6. Place in your air fryer and cook for 30 minutes at 180°C. Leave in the air fryer for 30 minutes whilst it cools
7. Refrigerate for 6 hours

Cherry Pies

Servings: 6
Cooking Time: xx
Ingredients:
- 300g prepared shortcrust pastry
- 75g cherry pie filling
- Cooking spray
- 3 tbsp icing sugar
- ½ tsp milk

Directions:
1. Cut out 6 pies with a cookie cutter
2. Add 1 ½ tbsp filling to each pie
3. Fold the dough in half and seal around the edges with a fork
4. Place in the air fryer, spray with cooking spray
5. Cook at 175°C for 10 minutes
6. Mix icing sugar and milk and drizzled over cooled pies to serve

Grain-free Millionaire's Shortbread

Servings: 9
Cooking Time: xx
Ingredients:
- BASE
- 60 g/5 tablespoons coconut oil
- 1 tablespoon maple syrup
- ½ teaspoon vanilla extract
- 180 g/1¾ cups ground almonds
- a pinch of salt
- MIDDLE
- 185 g/1⅓ cups dried pitted dates (soak in hot water for at least 20 minutes, then drain)
- 2 tablespoons almond butter
- 90 g/scant ½ cup canned coconut milk (the thick part once it has separated is ideal)
- TOPPING
- 125 g/½ cup coconut oil
- 4 tablespoons cacao powder
- 1 tablespoon maple syrup

Directions:
1. Preheat the air-fryer to 180°C/350°F.
2. To make the base, in a small saucepan melt the coconut oil with the maple syrup and vanilla extract. As soon as the coconut oil is melted, stir in the almonds and the salt off the heat. Press this mixture into a 15 x 15-cm/6 x 6-in. baking pan.
3. Add the baking pan to the preheated air-fryer and cook for 4 minutes, until golden brown on top. Remove from the air-fryer and allow to cool.
4. In a food processor, combine the rehydrated drained dates, almond butter and coconut milk. Once the base is cool, pour this mixture over the base and pop into the freezer to set for an hour.
5. After the base has had 45 minutes in the freezer, make the topping by heating the coconut oil in a saucepan until melted, then whisk in the cacao powder and maple syrup off the heat to make a chocolate syrup. Leave this to cool for 15 minutes, then pour over the set middle layer and return to the freezer for 30 minutes. Cut into 9 squares to serve.

Chocolate And Berry Pop Tarts

Servings: 8
Cooking Time: 10 Minutes
Ingredients:
- For the filling:
- 50 g / 1.8 oz fresh raspberries
- 50 g / 1.8 oz fresh strawberries
- 100 g / 3.5 oz granulated sugar
- 1 tsp corn starch
- For the pastry:
- 1 sheet puff pastry
- For the frosting:
- 4 tbsp powdered sugar
- 2 tbsp maple syrup or honey
- Chocolate sprinkles

Directions:
1. Preheat the air fryer to 180 °C / 350 °F and line the mesh basket with parchment paper or grease it with olive oil.
2. Make the filling by combining the strawberries, raspberries, and granulated sugar in a saucepan. Place on medium heat until the mixture starts to boil. When it begins to boil, turn the temperature down to a low setting. Use a spoon to break up the berries and forms a smooth mixture.
3. Stir in the corn starch and let the mixture simmer for 1-2 minutes. Remove the saucepan from the heat and set aside to cool while you prepare the pastry.
4. Roll out the large sheet of puff pastry and cut it into 8 equal rectangles.
5. Spoon 2 tbsp of the cooled berry filling onto one side of each rectangle. Fold over the other side of each puff pastry rectangle to cover the filling. Press the sides down with a fork or using your fingers to seal the filling into the pastry.
6. Transfer the puff pastry rectangles into the lined air fryer basket. Cook for 10-12 minutes until the pastry is golden and crispy.

7. Meanwhile, make the frosting. Whisk together the powdered sugar, maple syrup or honey, and chocolate chips in a bowl until well combined.

8. Carefully spread a thin layer of frosting in the centre of each pop tart. Allow the frosting to set before serving.

Mini Egg Buns

Servings: 8
Cooking Time:xx
Ingredients:
- 100g self raising flour
- 100g caster sugar
- 100g butter
- 2 eggs
- 2 tbsp honey
- 1 tbsp vanilla essence
- 300g soft cheese
- 100g icing sugar
- 2 packets of Mini Eggs

Directions:
1. Cream the butter and sugar together until light and fluffy, beat in the eggs one at a time
2. Add the honey and vanilla essence, fold in the flour a bit at a time
3. Divide the mix into 8 bun cases and place in the air fryer. Cook at 180°C for about 20 minutes
4. Cream the soft cheese and icing sugar together to make the topping
5. Allow the buns to cool, pipe on the topping mix and add mini eggs

Banana Maple Flapjack

Servings:9
Cooking Time:xx
Ingredients:
- 100 g/7 tablespoons butter (or plant-based spread if you wish)
- 75 g/5 tablespoons maple syrup
- 2 ripe bananas, mashed well with the back of a fork
- 1 teaspoon vanilla extract
- 240 g/2½ cups rolled oats/quick-cooking oats

Directions:
1. Gently heat the butter and maple syrup in a medium saucepan over a low heat until melted. Stir in the mashed banana, vanilla and oats and combine all ingredients. Pour the flapjack mixture into a 15 x 15-cm/6 x 6-in. baking pan and cover with foil.
2. Preheat the air-fryer to 200°C/400°F.
3. Add the baking pan to the preheated air-fryer and air-fry for 12 minutes, then remove the foil and cook for a further 4 minutes to brown the top. Leave to cool before cutting into 9 squares.

Sweet Potato Dessert Fries

Servings: 4
Cooking Time:xx
Ingredients:
- 2 sweet potatoes, peeled
- ½ tbsp coconut
- 1 tbsp arrowroot
- 2 tsp melted butter
- ½ cup coconut sugar
- 2 tsp cinnamon
- Icing sugar

Directions:
1. Cut the potatoes into ½ inch thick strips, coat in arrowroot and coconut oil
2. Place in the air fryer and cook at 190°C for 18 minutes shaking halfway through
3. Remove from air fryer and place in a bowl, drizzle with melted butter
4. Mix in sugar and cinnamon
5. Sprinkle with icing sugar to serve

Thai Fried Bananas

Servings: 8
Cooking Time:xx
Ingredients:
- 4 ripe bananas
- 2 tbsp flour
- 2 tbsp rice flour
- 2 tbsp cornflour
- 2 tbsp desiccated coconut
- Pinch salt
- ½ tsp baking powder
- ½ tsp cardamon powder

Directions:
1. Place all the dry ingredients in a bowl and mix well. Add a little water at a time and combine to form a batter
2. Cut the bananas in half and then half again length wise
3. Line the air fryer with parchment paper and spray with cooking spray
4. Dip each banana piece in the batter mix and place in the air fryer
5. Cook at 200°C for 10 -15 minutes turning halfway
6. Serve with ice cream

Pop Tarts

Servings: 6
Cooking Time: xx
Ingredients:
- 200g strawberries quartered
- 25g sugar
- ½ pack ready made pie crust
- Cooking spray
- 50g powdered sugar
- 1 ½ tsp lemon juice
- 1 tbsp sprinkles

Directions:
1. Stir together strawberries and sugar in a bowl
2. Allow to stand for 15 minutes then microwave on high for 10 minutes stirring halfway through
3. Roll out pie crust int0 12 inch circle, cut into 12 rectangles
4. Spoon mix onto 6 of the rectangles
5. Brush the edges with water and top with the remaining rectangles
6. Press around the edges with a fork to seal
7. Place in the air fryer and cook at 175ºC for about 10 minutes
8. Mix together powdered sugar and decorate add sprinkles

Chocolate Soufflé

Servings: 2
Cooking Time: xx
Ingredients:
- 150g semi sweet chocolate, chopped
- ¼ cup butter
- 2 eggs, separated
- 3 tbsp sugar
- ½ tsp vanilla extract
- 2 tbsp flour
- Icing sugar
- Whipped cream to serve

Directions:
1. Butter and sugar 2 small ramekins
2. Melt the chocolate and butter together
3. In another bowl beat the egg yolks, add the sugar and vanilla beat well
4. Drizzle in the chocolate mix well, add the flour and mix well
5. Preheat the air fryer to 165ºC
6. Whisk the egg whites to soft peaks, gently fold into the chocolate mix a little at a time
7. Add the mix to ramekins and place in the air fryer. Cook for about 14 minutes
8. Dust with icing sugar, serve with whipped cream

Coffee, Chocolate Chip, And Banana Bread

Servings: 8
Cooking Time: 1 Hour 10 Minutes
Ingredients:
- 200 g / 7 oz plain flour
- 1 tsp baking powder
- 1 tsp ground cinnamon
- 1 tbsp ground coffee
- ½ tsp salt
- 2 ripe bananas, peeled
- 2 eggs, beaten
- 100 g / 3.5 oz granulated sugar
- 50 g / 3.5 oz brown sugar
- 100 g / 3.5 oz milk chocolate chips
- 4 tbsp milk
- 2 tbsp olive oil
- 1 tsp vanilla extract

Directions:
1. Preheat the air fryer to 150 °C / 300 °F and line a loaf tin with parchment paper.
2. In a large mixing bowl, combine the plain flour, baking powder, ground cinnamon, and salt.
3. Mash the ripe bananas in a separate bowl until there are no lumps. Whisk in the beaten eggs, followed by the granulated sugar, brown sugar, and milk chocolate chips until well combined.
4. Stir in the milk, olive oil, and vanilla extract before combining the dry and wet ingredients. Mix until combined into one smooth mixture.
5. Pour the batter into the prepared loaf tin and transfer into the air fryer basket. Cook for 30-40 minutes until the cake is set and golden on top. Insert a knife into the centre of the cake. It should come out dry when the cake is fully cooked.
6. Remove the loaf tin from the air fryer and set aside to cool on a drying rack. Once cooled, remove the cake from the loaf tin and cut into slices.
7. Enjoy the cake hot or cold.

Peanut Butter & Chocolate Baked Oats

Servings:9
Cooking Time:xx
Ingredients:
- 150 g/1 heaped cup rolled oats/quick-cooking oats
- 50 g/⅓ cup dark chocolate chips or buttons
- 300 ml/1¼ cups milk or plant-based milk
- 50 g/3½ tablespoons Greek or plant-based yogurt
- 1 tablespoon runny honey or maple syrup
- ½ teaspoon ground cinnamon or ground ginger
- 65 g/scant ⅓ cup smooth peanut butter

Directions:
1. Stir all the ingredients together in a bowl, then transfer to a baking dish that fits your air-fryer drawer.
2. Preheat the air-fryer to 180ºC/350ºF.
3. Add the baking dish to the preheated air-fryer and air-fry for 10 minutes. Remove from the air-fryer and serve hot, cut into 9 squares.

Apple And Cinnamon Empanadas

Servings: 12
Cooking Time:xx
Ingredients:
- 12 empanada wraps
- 2 diced apples
- 2 tbsp honey
- 1 tsp vanilla extract
- 1 tsp cinnamon
- ⅛ tsp nutmeg
- Olive oil spray
- 2 tsp cornstarch
- 1 tsp water

Directions:
1. Place apples, cinnamon, honey, vanilla and nutmeg in a pan cook for 2-3 minutes until apples are soft
2. Mix the cornstarch and water add to the pan and cook for 30 seconds
3. Add the apple mix to each of the empanada wraps
4. Roll the wrap in half, pinch along the edges, fold the edges in then continue to roll to seal
5. Place in the air fryer and cook at 200ºC for 8 minutes, turn and cook for another 10 minutes

Shortbread Cookies

Servings: 2
Cooking Time:xx
Ingredients:
- 250g flour
- 75g sugar
- 175g butter
- 1 tbsp vanilla essence
- Chocolate buttons for decoration

Directions:
1. Preheat air fryer to 180ºC
2. Place all ingredients apart from the chocolate into a bowl and rub together
3. Form into dough and roll out. Cut into heart shapes using a cookie cutter
4. Place in the air fryer and cook for 10 minutes
5. Place the chocolate buttons onto the shortbread and cook for another 10 minutes at 160ºC

Pecan & Molasses Flapjack

Servings:9
Cooking Time:xx
Ingredients:
- 120 g/½ cup plus 2 teaspoons butter or plant-based spread, plus extra for greasing
- 40 g/2 tablespoons blackstrap molasses
- 60 g/5 tablespoons unrefined sugar
- 50 g/½ cup chopped pecans
- 200 g/1½ cups porridge oats/steelcut oats (not rolled or jumbo)

Directions:
1. Preheat the air-fryer to 180ºC/350ºF.
2. Grease and line a 15 x 15-cm/6 x 6-in. baking pan.
3. In a large saucepan melt the butter/spread, molasses and sugar. Once melted, stir in the pecans, then the oats. As soon as they are combined, tip the mixture into the prepared baking pan and cover with foil.
4. Place the foil-covered baking pan in the preheated air-fryer and air-fry for 10 minutes. Remove the foil, then cook for a further 2 minutes to brown the top. Leave to cool, then cut into 9 squares.

Sugar Dough Dippers

Servings: 12
Cooking Time:xx
Ingredients:
- 300g bread dough
- 75g melted butter
- 100g sugar
- 200ml double cream
- 200g semi sweet chocolate
- 2 tbsp amaretto

Directions:

1. Roll the dough into 2 15inch logs, cut each one into 20 slices. Cut each slice in half and twist together 2-3 times. Brush with melted butter and sprinkle with sugar
2. Preheat the air fryer to 150°C
3. Place dough in the air fryer and cook for 5 minutes, turnover and cook for a further 3 minutes
4. Place the cream in a pan and bring to simmer over a medium heat, place the chocolate chips in a bowl and pour over the cream
5. Mix until the chocolate is melted then stir in the amaretto
6. Serve the dough dippers with the chocolate dip

Oat-covered Banana Fritters

Servings: 4
Cooking Time:xx
Ingredients:
- 3 tablespoons plain/all-purpose flour (gluten-free if you wish)
- 1 egg, beaten
- 90 g/3 oz. oatcakes (gluten-free if you wish) or oat-based cookies, crushed to a crumb consistency
- 1½ teaspoons ground cinnamon
- 1 tablespoon unrefined sugar
- 4 bananas, peeled

Directions:
1. Preheat the air-fryer to 180°C/350°F.
2. Set up three bowls – one with flour, one with beaten egg and the other with the oatcake crumb, cinnamon and sugar mixed together. Coat the bananas in flour, then in egg, then in the crumb mixture.
3. Add the bananas to the preheated air-fryer and air-fry for 10 minutes. Serve warm.

Chocolate Orange Fondant

Servings: 4
Cooking Time:xx
Ingredients:
- 2 tbsp self raising flour
- 4 tbsp caster sugar
- 115g dark chocolate
- 115g butter
- 1 medium orange rind and juice
- 2 eggs

Directions:
1. Preheat the air fryer to 180°C and grease 4 ramekins
2. Place the chocolate and butter in a glass dish and melt over a pan of hot water, stir until the texture is creamy
3. Beat the eggs and sugar together until pale and fluffy
4. Add the orange and egg mix to the chocolate and mix
5. Stir in the flour until fully mixed together
6. Put the mix into the ramekins, place in the air fryer and cook for 12 minutes. Leave to stand for 2 minutes before serving

Apple Crumble

Servings: 4
Cooking Time:xx
Ingredients:
- 2 apples (each roughly 175 g/6 oz.), cored and chopped into 2-cm/¾-in cubes
- 3 tablespoons unrefined sugar
- 100 g/1 cup jumbo rolled oats/old-fashioned oats
- 40 g/heaped ¼ cup flour (gluten-free if you wish)
- 1 heaped teaspoon ground cinnamon
- 70 g/scant ⅓ cup cold butter, chopped into small cubes

Directions:
1. Preheat the air-fryer to 180°C/350°F.
2. Scatter the apple pieces in a baking dish that fits your air-fryer, then sprinkle over 1 tablespoon sugar. Add the baking dish to the preheated air-fryer and air-fry for 5 minutes.
3. Meanwhile, in a bowl mix together the oats, flour, remaining sugar and cold butter. Use your fingertips to bring the crumble topping together.
4. Remove the baking dish from the air-fryer and spoon the crumble topping over the partially cooked apple. Return the baking dish to the air dryer and air-fry for a further 10 minutes. Serve warm or cold.

Lemon Pies

Servings: 6
Cooking Time:xx
Ingredients:
- 1 pack of pastry
- 1 egg beaten
- 200g lemon curd
- 225g powdered sugar
- ½ lemon

Directions:
1. Preheat the air fryer to 180°C
2. Cut out 6 circles from the pastry using a cookie cutter
3. Add 1 tbsp of lemon curd to each circle, brush the edges with egg and fold over
4. Press around the edges of the dough with a fork to seal
5. Brush the pies with the egg and cook in the air fryer for 10 minutes

6. Mix the lemon juice with the powdered sugar to make the icing and drizzle on the cooked pies

Lemon Tarts

Servings: 8
Cooking Time:xx
Ingredients:
- 100g butter
- 225g plain flour
- 30g caster sugar
- Zest and juice of 1 lemon
- 4 tsp lemon curd

Directions:
1. In a bowl mix together butter, flour and sugar until it forms crumbs, add the lemon zest and juice
2. Add a little water at a time and mix to form a dough
3. Roll out the dough and line 8 small ramekins with it
4. Add ¼ tsp of lemon curd to each ramekin
5. Cook in the air fryer for 15 minutes at 180°C

Brazilian Pineapple

Servings: 2
Cooking Time:xx
Ingredients:
- 1 small pineapple, cut into spears
- 100g brown sugar
- 2 tsp cinnamon
- 3 tbsp melted butter

Directions:
1. Mix the brown sugar and cinnamon together in a small bowl
2. Brush the pineapple with melted butter
3. Sprinkle with the sugar and cinnamon
4. Heat the air fryer to 200°C
5. Cook the pineapple for about 10 minutes

Apple Chips With Yogurt Dip

Servings: 4
Cooking Time:xx
Ingredients:
- 1 apple
- 1 tsp cinnamon
- 2 tsp oil
- Cooking spray
- 25g greek yogurt
- 1 tbsp almond butter
- 1 tsp honey

Directions:
1. Thinly slice the apple, place in a bowl and coat with cinnamon and oil
2. Coat the air fryer with cooking spray and add the apple slices
3. Cook the slices for 12 minutes at 180°C
4. Mix the butter, honey and yogurt together and serve with the apple slices as a dip

Banana And Nutella Sandwich

Servings: 2
Cooking Time:xx
Ingredients:
- Softened butter
- 4 slices white bread
- 25g chocolate spread
- 1 banana

Directions:
1. Preheat the air fryer to 185°C
2. Spread butter on one side of all the bread slices
3. Spread chocolate spread on the other side of each slice
4. Add sliced banana to two slices of bread then add the other slice of bread to each
5. Cut in half diagonally to form triangles
6. Place in the air fryer and cook for 5 minutes turn over and cook for another 2 minutes

Crispy Snack Apples

Servings: 2
Cooking Time:xx
Ingredients:
- 3 apples, Granny Smith work best
- 250g flour
- 3 whisked eggs
- 25g sugar
- 1 tsp ground cinnamon
- 250g cracker crumbs

Directions:
1. Preheat the air fryer to 220°C
2. Peel the apples, remove the cores and cut into wedges
3. Take three bowls - the first with the flour, the second with the egg, and then this with the cracker crumbs, sugar and cinnamon combined
4. Dip the apple wedges into the egg in order
5. Place in the air fryer and cook for 5 minutes, turning over with one minute remaining

Strawberry Danish

Servings: 2
Cooking Time:xx
Ingredients:
- 1 tube crescent roll dough
- 200g cream cheese
- 25g strawberry jam
- 50g diced strawberries
- 225g powdered sugar
- 2-3 tbsp cream

Directions:
1. Roll out the dough
2. Spread the cream cheese over the dough, cover in jam
3. Sprinkle with strawberries
4. Roll the dough up from the short side and pinch to seal
5. Line the air fryer with parchment paper and spray with cooking spray
6. Place the dough in the air fryer and cook at 175°C for 20 minutes
7. Mix the cream with the powdered sugar and drizzle on top once cooked

Birthday Cheesecake

Servings: 8
Cooking Time:xx
Ingredients:
- 6 Digestive biscuits
- 50g melted butter
- 800g soft cheese
- 500g caster sugar
- 4 tbsp cocoa powder
- 6 eggs
- 2 tbsp honey
- 1 tbsp vanilla

Directions:
1. Flour a spring form tin to prevent sticking
2. Crush the biscuits and then mix with the melted butter, press into the bottom and sides of the tin
3. Mix the caster sugar and soft cheese with an electric mixer. Add 5 eggs, honey and vanilla. Mix well
4. Spoon half the mix into the pan and pat down well. Place in the air fryer and cook at 180°C for 20 minutes then 160°C for 15 minutes and then 150°C for 20 minutes
5. Mix the cocoa and the last egg into the remaining mix. Spoon over the over the bottom layer and place in the fridge. Chill for 11 hours

Grilled Ginger & Coconut Pineapple Rings

Servings: 4
Cooking Time:xx
Ingredients:
- 1 medium pineapple
- coconut oil, melted
- 1½ teaspoons coconut sugar
- ½ teaspoon ground ginger
- coconut or vanilla yogurt, to serve

Directions:
1. Preheat the air-fryer to 180°C/350°F.
2. Peel and core the pineapple, then slice into 4 thick rings.
3. Mix together the melted coconut oil with the sugar and ginger in a small bowl. Using a pastry brush, paint this mixture all over the pineapple rings, including the sides of the rings.
4. Add the rings to the preheated air-fryer and air-fry for 20 minutes. Check after 18 minutes as pineapple sizes vary and your rings may be perfectly cooked already. You'll know they are ready when they're golden in colour and a fork can easily be inserted with very little resistance
5. Serve warm with a generous spoonful of yogurt.

Lava Cakes

Servings: 4
Cooking Time:xx
Ingredients:
- 1 ½ tbsp self raising flour
- 3 ½ tbsp sugar
- 150g butter
- 150g dark chocolate, chopped
- 2 eggs

Directions:
1. Preheat the air fryer to 175°C
2. Grease 4 ramekin dishes
3. Melt chocolate and butter in the microwave for about 3 minutes
4. Whisk the eggs and sugar together until pale and frothy
5. Pour melted chocolate into the eggs and stir in the flour
6. Fill the ramekins ¾ full, place in the air fryer and cook for 10 minutes

APPENDIX A: Measurement

BASIC KITCHEN CONVERSIONS & EQUIVALENTS DRY MEASUREMENTS CONVERSION CHART

3 TEASPOONS = 1 TABLESPOON = 1/16 CUP

6 TEASPOONS = 2 TABLESPOONS = 1/8 CUP

12 TEASPOONS = 4 TABLESPOONS = 1/4 CUP

24 TEASPOONS = 8 TABLESPOONS = 1/2 CUP

36 TEASPOONS = 12 TABLESPOONS = 3/4 CUP

48 TEASPOONS = 16 TABLESPOONS = 1 CUP

METRIC TO US COOKING CONVERSIONS OVEN TEMPERATURES

120 ° C = 250 ° F 160 ° C = 320 ° F 180° C = 350 ° F 205 ° C = 400 ° F 220 ° C = 425 ° F

LIQUID MEASUREMENTS CONVERSION CHART

8 FLUID OUNCES = 1 CUP = 1/2 PINT = 1/4 QUART

16 FLUID OUNCES = 2 CUPS = 1 PINT = 1/2 QUART

32 FLUID OUNCES = 4 CUPS = 2 PINTS = 1 QUART = 1/4 GALLON

128 FLUID OUNCES = 16 CUPS = 8 PINTS = 4 QUARTS = 1 GALLON

BAKING IN GRAMS

1 CUP FLOUR = 140 GRAMS

1 CUP SUGAR = 150 GRAMS

1 CUP POWDERED SUGAR = 160 GRAMS

1 CUP HEAVY CREAM = 235 GRAMS

VOLUME

1 MILLILITER = 1/5 TEASPOON

5 ML = 1 TEASPOON

15 ML = 1 TABLESPOON

240 ML = 1 CUP OR 8 FLUID OUNCES

1 LITER = 34 FL. OUNCES

WEIGHT

1 GRAM = .035 OUNCES

100 GRAMS = 3.5 OUNCES

500 GRAMS = 1.1 POUNDS

1 KILOGRAM = 35 OUNCES

US TO METRIC COOKING CONVERSIONS

1/5 TSP = 1 ML

1 TSP = 5 ML

1 TBSP = 15 ML

1 FL OUNCE = 30 ML

1 CUP = 237 ML

1 PINT (2 CUPS) = 473 ML

1 QUART (4 CUPS) = .95 LITER

1 GALLON (16 CUPS) = 3.8 LITERS

1 OZ = 28 GRAMS

1 POUND = 454 GRAMS

BUTTER

1 CUP BUTTER = 2 STICKS = 8 OUNCES = 230 GRAMS = 8 TABLESPOONS

WHAT DOES 1 CUP EQUAL

1 CUP = 8 FLUID OUNCES

1 CUP = 16 TABLESPOONS

1 CUP = 48 TEASPOONS

1 CUP = 1/2 PINT

1 CUP = 1/4 QUART

1 CUP = 1/16 GALLON

1 CUP = 240 ML

BAKING PAN CONVERSIONS

1 CUP ALL-PURPOSE FLOUR = 4.5 OZ

1 CUP ROLLED OATS = 3 OZ 1 LARGE EGG = 1.7 OZ

1 CUP BUTTER = 8 OZ 1 CUP MILK = 8 OZ

1 CUP HEAVY CREAM = 8.4 OZ

1 CUP GRANULATED SUGAR = 7.1 OZ

1 CUP PACKED BROWN SUGAR = 7.75 OZ

1 CUP VEGETABLE OIL = 7.7 OZ

1 CUP UNSIFTED POWDERED SUGAR = 4.4 OZ

BAKING PAN CONVERSIONS

9-INCH ROUND CAKE PAN = 12 CUPS

10-INCH TUBE PAN = 16 CUPS

11-INCH BUNDT PAN = 12 CUPS

9-INCH SPRINGFORM PAN = 10 CUPS

9 X 5 INCH LOAF PAN = 8 CUPS

9-INCH SQUARE PAN = 8 CUPS

APPENDIX B: Recipes Index

A

Air-fried Artichoke Hearts 35
Almond Green Beans 74
Almond Topped Trout 56
Antipasto-stuffed Cherry Tomatoes 27
Apple And Cinnamon Empanadas 87
Apple And Cinnamon Puff Pastry Pies 83
Apple Chips With Yogurt Dip 89
Apple Crumble 88
Apple French Toast Sandwich 23
Apricot-cheese Mini Pies 19
Arancini 39
Aromatic Pork Tenderloin 51
Artichoke Samosas 26
Asian Five-spice Wings 29
Asian Rice Logs 32
Asian-style Orange Chicken 70
Aubergine Dip 34
Authentic Sausage Kartoffel Salad 46
Avocado Toast With Lemony Shrimp 29
Avocado Toasts With Poached Eggs 21

B

Baby Back Ribs 52
Bacon & Blue Cheese Tartlets 25
Bacon & Egg Quesadillas 17
Bacon-wrapped Asparagus 80
Bacon-wrapped Filets Mignons 51
Bagel Pizza 35
Bagels With Avocado & Tomatoes 16
Baharat Lamb Kebab With Mint Sauce 43
Baked Aubergine Slices With Yogurt Dressing 34
Baked Shishito Peppers 81
Balsamic Grape Dip 33
Balsamic London Broil 48
Banana And Nutella Sandwich 89
Banana Maple Flapjack 85
Barbecue Country-style Pork Ribs 52
Beef & Spinach Sauté 53
Beef Al Carbon (street Taco Meat) 48

Beef Steak Sliders 28
Beer-breaded Halibut Fish Tacos 60
Better-than-chinese-take-out Sesame Beef 45
Birthday Cheesecake 90
Blackened Catfish 61
Blueberry Pannenkoek (dutch Pancake) 23
Boneless Ribeye Steaks 51
Brazilian Pineapple 89
Breaded Mozzarella Sticks 30
Breakfast Chimichangas 16
Breakfast Frittata 22
Breakfast Sausage Bites 16
Brie And Cranberry Burgers 43
Broccoli Cheese 37
Broccoli Cornbread 19
Buffalo Chicken Wontons 66
Buffalo French Fries 31
Butternut Squash Falafel 37
Butternut Squash–wrapped Halibut Fillets 57
Buttery Radish Wedges 77

C

Cajun Breakfast Potatoes 15
Cajun Chicken Livers 69
Cajun Fried Chicken 64
California Burritos 49
Calzones South Of The Border 42
Camembert & Soldiers 36
Carne Asada Recipes 44
Catalan-style Crab Samfaina 57
Cauliflower "tater" Tots 28
Charred Chicken Breasts 66
Charred Radicchio Salad 82
Charred Shishito Peppers 29
Cheese & Crab Stuffed Mushrooms 56
Cheese Arancini 27
Cheese Straws 31
Cheese-rice Stuffed Bell Peppers 73
Cheesy Chicken Tenders 65
Cheesy Mushroom-stuffed Pork Loins 44
Cherry Pies 84
Chicken Adobo 64
Chicken And Cheese Chimichangas 66
Chicken Cordon Bleu 63
Chicken Flatbread Pizza With Spinach 68
Chicken Flautas 72
Chicken Fried Rice 69

Chicken Fried Steak 48
Chicken Nachos 25
Chicken Souvlaki Gyros 65
Chicken Tikka Masala 71
Chickpea And Sweetcorn Falafel 36
Chilean-style Chicken Empanadas 64
Chili Black Bean Empanadas 26
Chili Blackened Shrimp 59
Chili Corn On The Cob 28
Chili Pepper Popcorn 24
Chocolate Almond Crescent Rolls 22
Chocolate And Berry Pop Tarts 84
Chocolate Orange Fondant 88
Chocolate Soufflé 86
Cholula Avocado Fries 25
Christmas Chicken & Roasted Grape Salad 63
Cilantro Sea Bass 60
Cinnamon Honeyed Pretzel Bites 31
Classic Chicken Cobb Salad 71
Classic Chicken Wings 27
Classic Crab Cakes 60
Classic Potato Chips 33
Coconut Chicken With Apricot-ginger Sauce 67
Coconut Shrimp Recipes 59
Coffee, Chocolate Chip, And Banana Bread 86
Corn Dog Bites 24
Courgette Burgers 40
Crispy Cornish Hen 66
Crispy Pierogi With Kielbasa And Onions 42
Crispy Pork Escalopes 46
Crispy Snack Apples 89
Crunchy Chicken Tenders 63
Crunchy Flounder Gratin 59
Crunchy French Toast Sticks 18
Crunchy Granola Muffins 22

D

Daadi Chicken Salad 70
Delicious Juicy Pork Meatballs 49
Dilly Red Snapper 53

E

Easy Carnitas 44
Easy Tex-mex Chimichangas 50
Easy Vanilla Muffins 17
Easy-peasy Shrimp 57

Effortless Toffee Zucchini Bread 15
Egg & Bacon Pockets 21
English Scones 14
Exotic Pork Skewers 42
Extra Crispy Country-style Pork Riblets 47

F

Family Chicken Fingers 70
Fancy Chicken Piccata 72
Farmers Market Quiche 13
Filled Mushrooms With Crab & Cheese 53
Firecracker Popcorn Shrimp 54
Flat Mushroom Pizzas 39
Flounder Fillets 56
Fried Cauliflower With Parmesan Lemon Dressing 80
Fried Corn On The Cob 76
Fried Eggplant Balls 80
Fried Green Tomatoes With Sriracha Mayo 78
Fried Pearl Onions With Balsamic Vinegar And Basil 79
Fried Pickles With Homemade Ranch 26

G

Garlic Bread Knots 21
Garlic Parmesan Bread Ring 15
Garlic-buttered Rib Eye Steak 47
Garlic-cheese Biscuits 21
Garlic-lemon Steamer Clams 58
German-style Pork Patties 46
Glazed Carrots 76
Glazed Meatloaf 49
Gnocchi Caprese 36
Goat Cheese Stuffed Portobellos 75
Goat Cheese, Beet, And Kale Frittata 20
Grain-free Millionaire's Shortbread 84
Greek Pita Pockets 47
Greek-inspired Ratatouille 74
Green Dip With Pine Nuts 73
Green Egg Quiche 17
Green Onion Pancakes 19
Grilled Ginger & Coconut Pineapple Rings 90
Ground Beef Calzones 45
Gruyère Asparagus & Chicken Quiche 68

H

Halibut Quesadillas 61
Halibut With Coleslaw 54
Ham And Cheddar Gritters 20
Hazelnut-crusted Fish 62
Herb-crusted Sole 58
Herb-marinated Chicken 64
Herb-rubbed Salmon With Avocado 54
Herby Breaded Artichoke Hearts 32
Herby Prawn & Zucchini Bake 55
Holiday Breakfast Casserole 14
Homemade French Fries 25
Homemade Pork Gyoza 52
Home-style Fish Sticks 62
Home-style Reuben Spread 31
Honey Lemon Thyme Glazed Cornish Hen 69
Honey Mustard Pork Roast 50
Honey Oatmeal 13
Honey Tater Tots With Bacon 33
Horseradish Crusted Salmon 57
Horseradish Tuna Croquettes 55
Hot Avocado Fries 30
Hot Cheese Bites 32
Hot Okra Wedges 81
Hot Shrimp 30
Indian Chicken Tandoori 67
Italian Breaded Eggplant Rounds 82
Italian Herb Stuffed Chicken 68
Italian-inspired Chicken Pizzadillas 65
Kale & Rice Chicken Rolls 67
Kid's Flounder Fingers 62
King Prawns Al Ajillo 58

L

Lava Cakes 90
Lemon Buns 83
Lemon Pies 88
Lemon Tarts 89
Lentil Balls With Zingy Rice 35
Lentil Burgers 40
Light Frittata 13
Lime Bay Scallops 56
Lobster Tails With Lemon Garlic Butter 61

M

Malaysian Shrimp With Sambal Mayo 55
Maple-peach And Apple Oatmeal 14
Mascarpone Iced Cinnamon Rolls 18
Mashed Potato Tots 79
Mexican-style Roasted Corn 78
Mini Egg Buns 85
Mini Quiche 37
Mushroom Pasta 35

N

New York Cheesecake 83

O

Oat-covered Banana Fritters 88
Orange Zingy Cauliflower 39

P

Paneer Tikka 38
Peanut Butter & Chocolate Baked Oats 87
Pecan & Molasses Flapjack 87
Pop Tarts 86

R

Rainbow Vegetables 37
Ratatouille 34
Roast Cauliflower & Broccoli 40
Roasted Brussels Sprouts With Bacon 73

S

Satay Chicken Skewers 71
Shortbread Cookies 87
Spiced Pumpkin Wedges 75
Spiced Roasted Acorn Squash 81
Spicy Spanish Potatoes 40
Spinach And Egg Air Fryer Breakfast Muffins 38
Spinach And Feta Croissants 40
Spring Ratatouille 38
Sticky Tofu With Cauliflower Rice 36
Strawberry Danish 90
Stuffed Avocados 76
Stunning Apples & Onions 78
Succulent Roasted Peppers 77

Sugar Dough Dippers 87
Sweet Potato Dessert Fries 85
Sweet Potato Taquitos 38

T

Thai Fried Bananas 85
Toasted Choco-nuts 77
Tofu & Broccoli Salad 81
Truffle Vegetable Croquettes 74

V

Vegan Fried Ravioli 41
Vegetarian "chicken" Tenders 39
Veggie Bakes 34
Veggie Fritters 75

W

Whole Wheat Pizza 41

Y

Yellow Squash 77

Z

Za'atar Bell Peppers 73

Printed in Great Britain
by Amazon